JEFF LOWENTHAL AND ROBERT SCHAFFNER

# FLEETWOOD MAC
## IN CHICAGO
### JANUARY 4TH
### 1969
THE LEGENDARY
## Chess Blues Session

Forewords by Mike Vernon MBE, and Marshall Chess

SCHIFFER PUBLISHING

4880 Lower Valley Road • Atglen, PA 19310

Stu Black, Mike Vernon,
Jeremy Spencer

PRINTS OF ANY OF THE IMAGES IN THIS BOOK CAN BE ORDERED
DIRECTLY FROM THE PHOTOGRAPHER.

HE CAN BE CONTACTED AT: COLLECTORPRINTS@GMAIL.COM

Library of Congress Control Number: 2022932582

Designed by Christopher Bower
Cover design by Molly Shields
Type set in Novecento sans wide/Adobe Garamond Pro

ISBN: 978-0-7643-6495-2
Printed in India

Published by Schiffer Publishing, Ltd.
4880 Lower Valley Road
Atglen, PA 19310
Phone: (610) 593-1777; Fax: (610) 593-2002
Email: Info@schifferbooks.com
Web: www.schifferbooks.com

For our complete selection of fine books on this and related subjects, please visit
our website at www.schifferbooks.com. You may also write for a free catalog.

Schiffer Publishing's titles are available at special discounts for bulk purchases
for sales promotions or premiums. Special editions, including personalized
covers, corporate imprints, and excerpts, can be created in large quantities
for special needs. For more information, contact the publisher.

We are always looking for people to write books on new and related
subjects. If you have an idea for a book, please contact us at proposals@
schifferbooks.com.

# DEDICATIONS

## JEFF LOWENTHAL

To my children, Dana and Graham, and my grandchildren, Payton, Brenden, and Melina

## ROBERT SCHAFFNER

For my family, Drew and Carol

# CONTENTS

# Fleetwood Mac in Chicago

# FOREWORD

BY MIKE VERNON, MBE
PRODUCER, *FLEETWOOD MAC IN CHICAGO*

Mike Vernon

This extraordinary and unique collection of photographs celebrates one day in the early recording career of the British blues entity known as Fleetwood Mac. The day in question was a Saturday. The date was January 4, 1969. The session took place at Chess Ter-Mar Studios, 320 E. 21st Street, in Chicago, and threw together the five members of the band—Peter Green, Jeremy Spencer, Danny Kirwan, John McVie, and Mick Fleetwood—with a handful of leading Chicago bluesmen: Buddy Guy, Otis Spann, Walter Horton, J. T. Brown, David "Honeyboy" Edwards, Willie Dixon, and S. P. Leary.

To the best of my knowledge, this was the first and *only* time that a "top-line" British blues band was to be recorded in an American studio with a group of "top-line" Afro-American blues musicians. The resultant musical endeavours—*Blues Jam at Chess*, a.k.a. *Fleetwood Mac in Chicago*— might not have reached the levels we could have hoped for, but the subsequent album releases from that memorable day have become highly prized by all those who jointly call themselves blues *and* Fleetwood Mac fans. So how did this event come to be, you may ask. Some interesting historical facts follow for the uninitiated.

During the latter part of 1967, Peter Green's Fleetwood Mac signed a recording deal with the UK-based independent blues label Blue Horizon. A debut single hit the streets in December 1967, while their eponymous album was launched early in 1968; that album shot up the UK charts to reach the #4 spot. A few months later, their second single—"Black Magic Woman"—entered the charts and climbed to #37.

The band's second album, *Mr. Wonderful*, reached the #10 slot during late spring of that year, while their third single—a cover of Little Willie John's classic "Need Your Love So Bad"—scrambled to #31 in July. But it was the instrumental "Albatross" that was to sweep all else aside when it hit the #1 slot on December 10 of that same year. Such success chartwise had never been expected—indeed never even discussed! In all previous recording sessions, we had taken the option to record as if being in the studio was a gig. No overdubs—just go for it until everyone was satisfied with the performance. But with "Albatross" we decided to layer to help create the desired aural atmosphere that was deemed to be perfection for such a worthy melody. Including the final mix-down we took two days in the studio getting it just right—and look what happened! As Peter Green commented to me in an interview with Jet Martin Celmins in June 1999: "I never expected it. Before you have a hit record, you really don't expect one to come." I responded: "And remember, for nearly a month after its release, it didn't happen . . . it was only when Top of the Pops played a snatch

of it at the very end of the show, as the credits came up, that the BBC got interested—and then you were booked for Dee Time and things took off from there." The sad thing was that the band never got to appear live on Top of the Pops (performing that tune). They were otherwise occupied in the USA.

The band's management, in conjunction with the Blue Horizon New York City office (headed by Seymour Stein and Richie Gottehrer) and Epic Records US, had been working on a plan to get Fleetwood Mac into the States to promote the release of their US debut album, *English Rose*. Every effort was made to pull together sufficient engagements to make it viable to undertake a tour that would last about six weeks—not an easy task, especially since there seemed to be reticence on the part of many promoters to take a chance on an unknown British blues band. John Mayall, Savoy Brown, and Ten Years After—no problem. But a hard-hitting, straight-ahead blues unit—one minute sounding like Elmore James and then the next like B.B. King—and with no stateside chart action. Too much like coals from Newcastle, maybe?

Mike Vernon, Peter Green, Mick Fleetwood, Jeremy Spencer, Buddy Guy

7

Honeyboy Edwards, Mike Vernon, Peter Green

But in any event, with a lot of hard work and not a little luck, a tour was announced. Fleetwood Mac would arrive in NYC on December 1, 1968, and play at a number of smaller venues in the Big Apple, as well as a three-night stretch at Steve Paul's Scene Club between 8th and 11th. They would then travel to Austin, Dallas, and Houston before returning to the East Coast for three consecutive nights at Boston's Tea Party. The band would then visit Detroit, Hallandale (Florida), and Philadelphia before arriving in Chicago on New Year's Day 1969.

That night, the band was scheduled to play at the Kinetic Playground supporting the Byrds and Muddy Waters. They would also support B.B. King at the Regal Theater the following night. On the third and fourth of January they would return to the Kinetic Playground to hook up again with Muddy and his band. The tenth of January would see the guys traveling

to the West Coast—Vancouver, Los Angeles, Fresno, and Sacramento, among a host of other places—before ending up in Pontiac, Michigan, for two shows on February 8 and 9. End of tour and back to Blighty.

Once I had been made aware of the tour schedule, I began to mull over ideas for potential recording activities that might be feasible if there were to be any on that list of free dates. Now, Peter himself had talked about traveling to the States, so he might have the opportunity to play in Chicago with the local "real deal" musos. An interesting concept, but probably tricky to put into practice. I talked to Seymour Stein and he suggested the possibility of doing some recording in Chicago at the Chess Brothers' studio complex. I had already had the pleasure of working at Ter-Mar in June 1968, when I produced material for Blue Horizon with Otis Spann, Sunnyland Slim, and Johnny Shines. Those sessions had proven to be highly

Buddy Guy, Mike Vernon

Peter Green, Danny Kirwan

Jeremy Spencer, Mike Vernon

rewarding—not least because I had been afforded the opportunity to work with the one and only Willie Dixon. Perhaps then it would be a smart move to involve Willie again in this new project? Seymour and I both agreed that that would be an excellent ploy.

Seymour subsequently had dialogue with Marshall Chess—son of Leonard Chess—about possible studio availability during the first week of January 1969. Yes indeed, there would be availability on the first Saturday of that month, and Marshall also confirmed that Willie was happy to act as the catalyst to search out the most-likely Chicago musicians who would be available for that date. I did send

Willie a personal wish list that included a number of seriously famous musicians—Buddy Guy, Otis Rush, Magic Sam, and Otis Spann, for instance. Not unexpectedly, though, many of those on that list were not available for one reason or another. I knew it would be a tough call to get commitments from many of the topflight artists who were working out of the Windy City, but I was thrilled to get a positive feedback via Willie that Otis Spann, J. T. Brown, Walter "Shakey" Horton, and Buddy Guy would be making an appearance. With the aforementioned commitments "in the bag," so to speak, it was time to firm up these on-hold plans with the members of Fleetwood Mac.

Initially, I recall there being an air of indifference wafting in from the general direction of certain band members, but both Peter and Jeremy seemed genuinely excited about the planned event. Peter had been a big fan of Otis Spann's work for some time, and mainly as a result of having heard his recordings with Muddy Waters. Jeremy was acting as if he had won the lottery as he began to relish the upcoming opportunity of recording with saxophonist J. T. Brown, who, for many years, had worked and recorded with his idol and main influence, Elmore James. Danny seemed to be slightly in a daze, while Messrs. McVie and Fleetwood continued to show a certain reticence about the project. Gradually, though, they began to warm to the idea, and when the time finally came to take care of business, they did exactly that!

My longtime friend Neil Slaven reminded me that we both traveled together from London to New York City on Christmas Eve, to spend the festive period with Seymour and Richie. The weather was very cold, and since there was a music festival going on in Hallandale, Florida, on the twenty-eighth that would be featuring Fleetwood Mac, Seymour decided to pay for us to fly south to the warmer climes of Miami. Indeed, when we

arrived both the heat and humidity were over 80 degrees. Some days later—Neil believes probably January 3 of the New Year—we jetted into Chicago, where the temperature was around minus 6 with snow on the ground! We checked into a hotel that was close to the Kinetic Playground in Uptown, and later that evening caught the band's show with the Byrds and Muddy Waters. Both of us recall standing in the audience next to Muddy's band members while they cheered Fleetwood Mac on. This enthusiasm—especially on the part of Otis Spann—did not go unnoticed.

The morning of Saturday, January 4 found Neil and me at Ter-Mar. It was great to see engineer Stu Black again and also to finally meet with Marshall. It was not long before musicians began drifting in to set up their equipment. I was then introduced to photographer Jeff Lowenthal, who was there at the suggestion of Marshall and for whom Jeff had done previous studio work. Smart move, since I have to admit to having totally forgotten about getting in a photographer! The results of his work can be seen in this fabulous collection. Only a limited number have been seen before, and almost exclusively those were part of the original artwork of the released vinyl analog albums already mentioned earlier.

Willie Dixon, Mike Vernon

11

Jeremy Spencer, Buddy Guy

As I recall, Jeff worked very quietly and unobtrusively while music was being created. When there was a studio monitor playback, he worked his magic. You can learn so much about a musician's inner feelings as they listen back to their individual performances. How does the saying go? "A picture is worth a thousand words" (F. R. Bernard, 1921). And now we get the opportunity to see the very best of those shots taken on that day fifty-two years ago. For those readers who have access to the analog vinyl or digital formats (or both) of the two volumes that make up the sum total of the audio from that day, you now have a decidedly clearer pictorial record to go with it—and no magnifying glasses required either! What more could you wish for? Sorry—no film.

Memories from that day back in 1969 are still quite vivid in my mind. Factually we probably didn't record more than two and a half hours' worth of music, and only on a couple of occasions did we record two takes of *any* tune. We probably didn't get started until midday or maybe even later. As for the finishing time—I have no idea. The band was scheduled to play again that same night at the Kinetic Playground, so if I was to make an educated guess I would say at the latest 9:00 p.m. Democracy reigned throughout the session, and when a decision was finally taken on what to record next and who would feature, everyone jumped in and got on with it. Roll the tape and push the record button was the order of the day. In general, though, I would say the atmosphere was fairly laid back. There was no real sense of urgency until the clock started winding down, when I did push Peter and the lads to try to get a couple of extra tunes on tape before time ran out on us. I am fairly certain that "Sugar Mama" and "Homework" closed the proceedings.

Whatever the resultant lack of commercial rewards earned from these unique Chicago recordings, they were, in their own way, a landmark. They represent the last occasion that Fleetwood Mac would record any straight-ahead blues material; the recording session held five days later in New York with featured vocalist/pianist Otis Spann did not include either Jeremy Spencer or Mick Fleetwood. Almost immediately following that day, further time was booked at Tempo Sound, and the beginnings of *Man of the World* were laid to tape. We agreed to meet up as soon as possible once the band was back in England—early February. Further guitar and vocal parts were added, and then we received the news from the band's manager that Blue Horizon no longer had a valid recording contract with FM.

As a gesture of good will, we could complete the recording of the current work and release it on Blue Horizon. Of course that did *not* come to pass. Immediate picked up the rights for that single, with the offer of a big-money deal. That deal never came to fruition, and although the single peaked on the charts at #2 during late spring, the company went, almost immediately, out of business. Fleetwood Mac were subsequently signed by Warner Brothers / Reprise, and the follow-up, "Oh Well," also sped to the #2 spot on October 4, 1969, continuing the run of Top 10 hit singles in the UK. It was at around that period of time that my brother Richard and I finally decided to market the best selections from that Chicago all-star "jam" session as a double-album release with a gatefold sleeve. *Blues Jam at Chess*

was not, it has to be said, met with a great deal of enthusiasm by the popular press, but the diehard blues fans were loving it! I don't think the band members were overenthusiastic either, and management was certainly not, but the masters belonged to us and we felt it to be the right time to air them.

Many years later, Peter Green, in that same interview with Martin Celmins, was quoted as saying, "I was never able to play in that studio"—referring, I would assume, to the vast size of the place. That didn't seem to bother the other musicians too much. Peter continued in the vein of "I played really well later that night at Pepper's Lounge"—actually Smitty's Corner, Neil and I believe. Well, that's true—an enthusiastic audience can make a big difference to a musician's performance. There *were* a few friends, relatives, and fans in attendance, though, on that long-ago Saturday afternoon. Maybe we could have invited more. Too late now.

# FOREWORD

## BY MARSHALL CHESS
## PRODUCER, *FLEETWOOD MAC IN CHICAGO*

It was 1969. I was twenty-seven years old, one of the first of the second-generation record men, so when Mike Vernon and Seymour Stein contacted me about doing a Fleetwood Mac blues album at Chess studios in Chicago, I instantly was on board. I loved the idea and did everything I could to make it happen.

At that time, expanding the Chess blues LP sales to new white blues lovers was my main job. I felt the *Blues Jam in Chicago* concept was a winner. My initial job was rounding up all the Chess artists and musicians This was a new kind of project for them, and I had to convince them that they would be paid. I remember that they ended up loving with playing with Fleetwood Mac. Everyone was impressed with the way they played the blues . . . especially Peter Green's guitar playing.

I recently played the albums to stoke my memories, and they sounded as good today as they did in 1969.

Mike Vernon, Marshall Chess in control room

Jeremy Spencer, Buddy Guy

# INTRODUCTION

## BY JEFF LOWENTHAL

This book has been more than fifty years in the making. Many events have transpired over those years, and I'd like to give you a little history of how I ended up to be the lucky guy to photograph this classic recording session.

While I later made my living as a *Newsweek* staff photographer, what I really liked to do was photograph musicians. I discovered this when, in my short career as a jazz disc jockey, I was instrumental in clarinetist and tenor saxophonist Franz Jackson getting a recording session, and I was invited to be a guest. I thought it would be a great idea to document the proceedings, since a number of excellent but rarely recorded players were to be involved.

The studio was a small one, run by a man who made records for what were called "hi-fi demonstration." It was in his garage, and dark. Nevertheless, I shot a few rolls and developed them myself.

Unhappy with the negatives, I mentioned this to a friend in public relations, and she said, "You should take them to a professional lab, like Astra Photo Service." Astra was a unique business in those days, a custom lab catering to journalistic photographers. They were able to produce good prints from my underexposed negatives, thanks to expert printer Ted Williams (also an excellent music photographer, who taught me a lot).

Two years later, Franz got a record date with a bigger company, Mercury Records. Again, I was invited, in thanks for having a part in their getting the original session. This one was held at Universal Recording Studios, a state-of-the-art facility that was larger and well lit. I also had improved as a photographer, now had a Nikon camera, and was prepared to produce better images, which I did.

Another visitor at the session was Don Gold, the editor of *Down Beat* magazine, who was planning a story about the session. Unfortunately, his photographer never showed up, and he asked me to stop by his office when I got my proofs. "Sure," I said, not knowing what would happen.

The result was better than I could have imagined—a two-page photo layout in the next issue of *Down Beat*! And there was my credit, in boldface type above it all, my first national publication.

I was hooked, and I continued to photograph music whenever I could, in clubs and recording sessions.

When the opportunity to shoot sessions for Chess Records presented itself, I was ready. Previously, I had photographed mostly jazz players, but Chess had some of the greatest blues musicians, such as Muddy Waters, Howlin' Wolf, and Willie Dixon, men whose records and fame extended to the world.

In fact, many of the Chess players were more famous overseas than they were in the States.

I wasn't familiar with Fleetwood Mac, but when Marshall Chess asked me to photograph the session that producer Mike Vernon had arranged with some of those famous Chess artists, I agreed.

Now, people ask if I have any anecdotes about the session, because after all, I was there for all of it. But to their disappointment, I really don't. The reason is simple: I was good at this kind of photography because I had an unbreakable rule: the most important thing at a session is the *music*. So, I went about my work not interfering, while the musicians did theirs.

Photographing a recording session required balancing my need for access, and the band's need to produce music. If you have *The Complete Blue Horizon* set, there is a snippet of conversation between Mike Vernon and Peter Green: Peter asks if they can turn off the studio lights, and Mike says, "He's coming out again . . ." (meaning me!).Now, if it had come to

Jeff Lowenthal in Chess studio

a question of whether I would come out to continue *or* the lights being turned off, I would vote to spend a few more minutes in the control booth and let the band have its darkness. Looking at some of these images, I see we compromised, turning the lights *down* but not out.

With the jazz sessions I shot, there was usually interplay with the participants, because I knew them and had photographed them before. This wasn't the case with Fleetwood Mac, because they were from the UK, so I'd never met them. Nevertheless, I tried to establish rapport, which allowed me to shoot close with a wide-angle lens (as in the iconic picture of Peter), but in doing so I remained as unobtrusive as possible. I believe I was successful—there are very few images where a player notices me. You *do* see them interact with one another, though, and that's what I wanted to capture.

These photographs were made with Leicas, because they are almost silent in operation. The last thing you want to do at a recording session is ruin a take with a misplaced shutter click. Or, during a playback, break a musician's concentration. The Leicas were as quiet as you could get.

For those of you who are photographers, here's the equipment I used for these images: two Leica M2 camera bodies, a Summicron 35 mm, a Summicron 50 mm, a 21 mm Super Angulon, and a Canon 28 mm, modified to fit my Leicas. This may seem to be a small set of equipment, but I've found that having just enough equipment allows you to concentrate on the assignment without having to spend time deciding what cameras and lenses to use, thus possibly missing pictures.

Looking at the images I made of guests at the session, there are only a few. I can't tell you who they were, but I can say they were lucky to be there! For those who are still around, it's a happy memory. But now, you too can have a feeling for what the studio looked like, and the interplay between the musicians, many of whom are no longer with us.

Photography is said to capture moments in time. I hope you enjoy what I captured fifty-two years ago, and the words we've assembled from the many people who know this session was special!

The music, of course, speaks for itself.

# INTRODUCTION

## BY ROBERT SCHAFFNER

Peter Green, Danny Kirwan

"Hi, Robert. Anyone who has a picture of the greatest guitarist/ musician on earth as his cover photo is a friend of mine. Cheers. BT."

This is how I began my relationship with Bruce Thomas. He noticed Jeff Lowenthal's photograph of Peter Green on my Facebook page, and from those email exchanges my son suggested I should write to Peter Green, not about music but about this encounter with Bruce. Sadly, I never got the opportunity. This book is my "letter."

"Music is your own experience, your thoughts, your wisdom. If you don't live it, it won't come out of your horn."
—Charlie Parker

*Fleetwood Mac in Chicago* was recorded only months before the last Mac album Peter Green "officially" played on, *Then Play On*.

This book is a photographic tribute to that double-album set, *Fleetwood Mac in Chicago / Blues Jam at Chess*. When I was a kid, these records gave me real insight into being in a recording studio with a band. I listened intently to the breaks between the songs, the direction of the producer, the talk-back of the band. While listening to the recordings, I would look at the photos contained within the original gatefold of this album, and imagine being in the studio with the band. No Pro Tools here. No cutting and pasting. The performances come through with a sense of urgency and freshness that was masterfully aided by Michael Vernon's brilliant production and the unique ambience that Chess Studios added to the recordings. Chess Studios is where some of the most notable R&B songs ever recorded were laid down for posterity. Musicians such as Willie Dixon, Buddy Guy, Otis Spann, the Rolling Stones, Howlin' Wolf, Chuck Berry, Muddy Waters, Bo Diddley, Etta James, and many more.

"If music be the food of love, play on."
—*Twelfth Night*, William Shakespeare

Peter played oftentimes not even knowing what or how he played a specific solo, from something he felt deep within. It was special only for that moment in time. As guitarists go, Peter was the whole package. He could sing, compose, play harp; he was truly something special. He had that special tone that many a guitarist attributes to his 1959 Les Paul Sunburst. Three well-versed guitarists, who also contributed to this book, played Peter's 1959 Les Paul. I believe not one of them sounded like Peter Green.

An extraordinary instrument requires an extraordinary player. Peter himself said that without Danny, their most successful song, "Albatross," would not have happened. Danny had one of the absolute best vibratos of any guitarist of his time, and perhaps one of the best ever, without the use of the more modern-day guitar trickery. Adding to his arsenal is an angelic vocal quality that we saw blossom over time. It was Danny who introduced a pop sensibility to Fleetwood Mac along with Bob Welch. Danny deserves a great deal of credit for creating the bridge that moved Fleetwood Mac from a blues band into the powerhouse pop band that they became.

Many pop rock bands from the 1960s and 1970s were highly influenced by Fleetwood Mac. If you watch and listen to Pete Townshend at the recent tribute concert to Peter Green (2020), he plays a song from *Kiln House*, "Station Man" (1970). Of course, this was not a Peter Green song, but a tune penned by Danny Kirwan, Jeremy Spencer, and John McVie. He then plays the opening chords of the Who anthem "Won't Get Fooled Again" (1971) and states, "Now listen to 'Station Man'" [laughs]. I was dumbfounded. Jeremy Spencer's style and his emotion on *Fleetwood Mac in Chicago* is a tribute to his deep affection and respect for Elmore James and Robert Johnson. Jeremy may have been in his element more than any other members of the band, since he experienced a dream come true while playing alongside J. T. Brown.

While attending a Jeremy Spencer concert outside Chicago, my friend Paul Hamer introduced me to Jeff Lowenthal. In 2020, Jeff and I began forming the idea of working together on a photo book. During the 1960s, Jeff was the session photographer at Chess Studios and had an archive of photographs from that time period. Among many things, we discussed how Jeff's photos had been copied and used in publications from various media without crediting the photographer. At that point, the decision was obvious.

This book is to document Jeff's place in musical history, with photos of some of the best British and American blues musicians this world has ever known. The public will see many of these photos for the first time, and I believe they will become some of the most iconic images in blues and rock musical history. I am humbled to be a small part of it.

# Acknowledgments

## Jeff Lowenthal

First I would like to acknowledge my coauthor, Robert Schaffner. Without Robert's belief that more of these pictures should be seen, they would have remained in my files, being licensed only for various publications. He persisted, one day I said, "Yes," and here we are. And here's Bob, ever the Peter Green partisan, driving a custom green Audi with the license "GREENY7."

And Paul Hamer, who first brought to my notice that this session was of interest to so many people. He was right! Peter Green Fleetwood Mac group membership on Facebook as of July 2021: 13,600!

Thanks to Paul Natkin and Harriet Choice.

And the drum scans provided by the PrintLab. Scanning fifty-two-year-old transparencies and negatives is a challenge. Thanks Xander, for your dedication to high quality.

And Richard Orlando, author of *Love That Burns*. He has graciously allowed us to quote liberally from his books, and he has many of the anecdotes that I missed because I was busy shooting!

And last, I want to thank producers Michael Vernon, MBE, and Marshall Chess, and all the contributors to this book.

Thank you for your kindnesses, thoughts, and memories of Fleetwood Mac in Chicago.

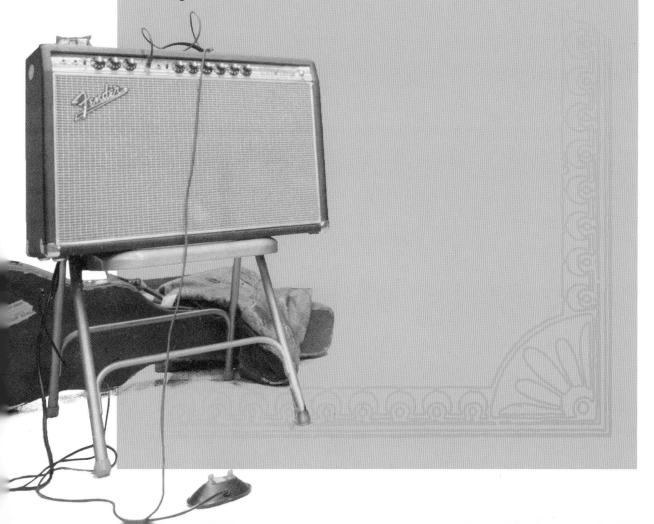

# Acknowledgments

## Robert Schaffner

Thanks to Jeff for this marvelous contribution to music history; Drew for "the spark"; Carol for "keep on keeping on"; Mike Vernon, MBE; Marshall Chess; Bruce Thomas; Aynsley Dunbar; Walter Trout; Kim Simmonds; Paul Hamer; Jol Dantzig; Dave Gregory; Michael Freeman; Martin Barre; Eric Corne; Jon Tiven; Steve Summers; Dea Matrona; Alan Clayson; Steve Matthes; Curtis Meissner; Richard Orlando; Bob Biondi, Schiffer Publishing; and Xander/PrintLab. And thank you to all of our contributors.

Thank you Peter Green [Baum] and Danny Kirwan for the music . . . it will always play on.

# FLEETWOOD MAC IN CHICAGO

Peter Green

## JOHN MAYALL

"I was blown away by Peter's strong personality and ferociously confident playing when he was in my band in the 1960s, and am so pleased that his legacy is being recognized and celebrated."

"Peter in his prime was without equal."

From Peter Green tribute, 2020

**John Mayall, OBE**

English blues singer, guitarist, organist, and songwriter, whose musical career spans over sixty years. In the 1960s, he was the founder of John Mayall & the Bluesbreakers, a band that has counted among its members some of the most famous blues and blues-rock musicians of the era.

Peter Green

# BRUCE THOMAS, INTERVIEW

**Michael Shelley**: It's amazing you cross paths with a bunch of amazing musicians . . . guys around the scene but still were accessible; I want to mention Peter Green.

**Bruce Thomas**: He touched a lot of people . . . not just the best guitar player, the best musician . . . to put it in perspective, I've kinda reevaluated it recently . . . Peter Green, I think, actually influenced my approach to playing music. His musicality and the way particularly that he honored the song and the melodic or harmonic content of the song and served the song. Rather than just blasting licks across it, like so many guitar heroes do, he played straight from the heart, without any barriers—it came directly from him! There is just no other musician or singer I can think of, apart from maybe Aretha Franklin, that could just deliver it from their inner self.

**MS**: It interesting [that] as a young man you were able to feel and have the sensitivity to see that.

**BT**: If you think about it, Peter Green was only nineteen years old at the time . . . where did his sensitivity [come] from—the supernatural or something like that? . . . I mean he's nineteen, twenty, and he is playing with the maturity of someone of several lifetimes. I guess there are certain people who just have their windows open to start with.

From podcast by Michael Shelley, WFMU, August 2020

"Peter Green played straight from his soul, through his heart, out through his fingers, through the strings and amplifier and into my ears and through my own heart to reach the same place in my soul that it came from in him, without any barriers or blockages—just a conduit that flowed straight through."

**Bruce Thomas**
Bassist, former Attraction (but still Attractive).

Shakey Horton, Buddy Guy, Peter Green

Danny Kirwan,
Peter Green

Peter Green, Willie Dixon

Willie Dixon

## KIM SIMMONDS, INTERVIEW

**Robert Schaffner**: Kim, we actually met a long time ago, when you lived in Croydon and you picked me and my friend up in your Jensen, and we drove back to your place and had a lengthy conversation, and you had me look at your stereo, because it wasn't getting any bass.

**Kim Simmonds**: Oh wow, now that you have mentioned those details, it's starting to come back to me.

**RS**: Well, Kim, you have been at it for over fifty years.

**KS**: I think it's about fifty-six years coming up; I started the band in the winter of 1965, and the only reason I know that is someone reminded me of that; they had found a newspaper clipping . . . otherwise, some of it is all a blank . . . it's surprising, I do remember more than one would think, but my problem is now I may remember it and then [it] goes right out of my mind and I forget it again.

**RS**: You had Michael Vernon as a producer, and I guess I never realized how many musicians you had in Savoy Brown that intersected with Fleetwood Mac or members of Fleetwood Mac.

**KS**: Well, that's interesting. Yeah, those people, Andy Sylvester and couple of others with Danny recorded Chris Youlden's first solo album.

**RS**: Those albums are some of my favorite Savoy Brown LPs; he was such a great singer.

**KS**: He was one of a kind, wasn't he? There was no one like him. I think Andy and Paul morphed into Danny's first album, I am assuming . . . Danny's album was after Chris's.

**RS**: Do you recall recording with Michael Vernon?

**KS**: Oh, of course! I don't think he did our singles . . . at the time he had a label called Purdah Records, and the first singles I did were for Purdah Records with him and his brother. The person who produced those was Neal Slavin; I think they were grouped together. The story is that I started a pub in Nags Head, a blues club, I started that in 1966. Mike came down to see the band because we were creating waves; that's where we created the Purdah singles . . . then from there, I don't recall, then Mike went over to Decca Records, then he recorded the John Mayall *Bluesbreakers* album at Decca, and then he recorded the Savoy Brown records at Decca. It's as clear as daylight those sessions we did with Mike. Then, by the time *Raw Sienna* came out with those Chris Youlden songs. I was feeling very full of my oats, so then I decided to do it for myself. That's when we departed Mike, and he probably was not too happy. I think at that point in time we were feeling more self-reliant more than anything. I have great admiration for Mike Vernon . . . he's wonderful!

**RS**: You played a lot of gigs with Fleetwood Mac; can you elaborate on those?

**KS**: Yeah, we did a whole lot of dates with them. The first time I saw them was at that club in Nags Head; I jammed with them. I put that place on the map, and it became the epicenter for blues, although you don't read about it much! So I must have been there for a year, through 1966 at least. I played there every Monday or Wednesday night. You know, sometimes when this stuff happened, you think you're making it up, but a guy from New Zealand posted to our Facebook page; he was British, but he said he was walking home in early 1966 near Nags Head and he hears this sound and thought, "It sounds like Muddy Water's Blues Band; what's this all about?" So he goes inside and there are about six people there, and it was Savoy Brown playing.

**RS**: Wow, what a compliment!

**KS**: Yeah, well, that first band was fabulous. It was probably the best if not one of the best Savoy Brown. It was so endearing to hear that story. By the time 1966 moved on, we were playing everywhere, and we vacated and it just became the place to go to pay the landlord or whoever was there and put on shows there. So the first time I saw Fleetwood Mac they were playing there. Went to see them and they were fabulous. The best thing I had ever seen!

**RS**: So at that time, Kirwan wasn't with them, right?

**KS**: No, Kirwan wasn't with them at that time. Then I did see them again, at Nags Head, with Kirwan—so that was the first time and [I] actually got to play with them. Then fast-forward to 1969 to Detroit; we did three or four nights with them—I distinctly remember that. Very influenced by Fleetwood

Danny Kirwan, Peter Green, Otis Spann, John McVie

Danny Kirwan, John McVie, Otis Spann, S. P. Leary, Mick Fleetwood, Peter Green

Mac . . . by their show, by Peter Green's guitar playing. Then quickly on to the 1972 time period. We did a big tour with Fleetwood Mac. I don't remember if Danny was in the band; Bob Weston was in the band. That reminds me that I don't think I ever said a word to Jeremy Spencer or Danny . . . ever. As a matter of fact, I don't recall Danny even being there. Spent a lot of time with Mick Fleetwood, and of course I knew him a long time ago too. He is a really good guy.

**RS**: Kim, I recall talking Fleetwood Mac with you in the 1970s, and one of the distinctive things I recall you saying is that Mick Fleetwood was a gentlemen.

**KS**; Oh, wow, isn't that nice, I can't even remember saying that.

**RS**: Sorry, I have a pretty good memory; lack of narcotics or something!

**KS**: [laughing] I did a few gigs with them when Stevie Nicks was in the band. So there's my Fleetwood Mac history.

**RS**: Many people talked about Peter's guitar, but some of the musicians I have spoken to said he could play any guitar and still would sound like Peter Green. You were a Gibson guy too, right?

**KS**: I still am; think I switched over from a Fender to a Gibson in 1968 or so. Peter was hugely influential on me. In fact our paths have crossed many times. Last I saw him, it was about ten years ago; we did a gig that my old keyboard player put together—a British blues giants or something. [*Note*: *The British Blues All Stars*, 2007, Blue Label]

**RS**: Yeah, it's a CD, right; I have it.

**KS**: It's a CD; I didn't know that. Peter was in the band, and we had a great time together. It was really a pleasure to be with him, because I am such an admirer of him. Because this was somewhat different than the past. His care provider brought him along to the show. He remembered a girlfriend I had in 1968 like it was yesterday. Well, there you go. I occasionally listen to that FMIC. There is only so much of the past I want to revisit. I do occasionally listen to it, and of course, it's brilliant. The British blues is really Chicago blues. We added, I think, a little extra energy to it. For Fleetwood Mac at the time, they were going back to pay homage, back to mecca or whatever you want to say. Chicago is where we all came from. I never seen as good a rhythm section as McVie and Fleetwood; they were just astonishing to me. They are just a powerhouse. I was looking at that time period when the Bluesbreakers got back together with McVie and Colin . . . watching their performance with McVie . . . what a good bass player! How inventive; he is just perfect for the part.

**Kim Simmonds**
Welsh guitarist, leader and founder member of the British blues-rock band Savoy Brown

John McVie

Peter Green, Danny Kirwan, John McVie

Peter Green

Honeyboy Edwards, Willie Dixon

# ERIC CORNE

The relationship between Chicago blues and British blues in the 1960s was an amazing thing. One fed the other and led to one of the most fruitful periods in music. John Mayall & the Bluesbreakers were of course at the center of this blues revival, often accompanying these blues legends on their European tours. So, it was quite fitting that Fleetwood Mac, born from the Bluesbreakers, would collaborate with some of the greats of Chicago blues and Chess Records. There's a relaxed spirit and spontaneity in these performances, with loads of great interplay. Peter Green was an astounding musician and singer; the economy of his playing and the sweetness of his tone have deservedly earned him a place as one of the greatest of all time. This recording is a special document, and it's great to see it richly expanded with this beautiful book of Jeff's photography.

**Eric Corne**
Founder and president of Forty Below Records; producer for John Mayall, Walter Trout, and Sugaray Rayford

Peter Green, John McVie

Danny Kirwan, John McVie, Peter Green, Stu Black

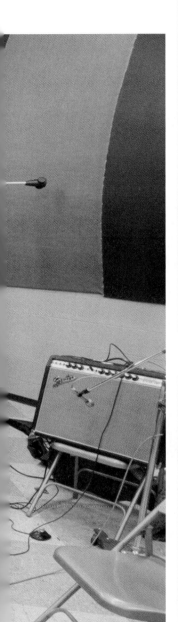

John McVie, Peter Green, Danny Kirwan

Danny Kirwan, Peter Green, John McVie, Shakey Horton

Otis Spann, John McVie

Peter Green, Danny Kirwan

## DAVE GREGORY

When those pictures first appeared in *Beat Instrumental* magazine, I was a sixteen-year-old kid still struggling to play. They were truly inspirational, as much for the instruments as the musicians; those vintage Les Paul guitars lit the spark that set me alight! It would take another sixteen years to find my first Gold Top, which took me a little closer to the source of "the sound." Peter and Danny together was an awesome pairing; so sad how it fell apart so quickly.

**Dave Gregory**
Guitarist, XTC, Tin Spirits, Big Big Train

Danny Kirwan, John
McVie, Mick Fleetwood

Danny Kirwan

Danny Kirwan, Peter Green, John McVie, Shakey Horton

# ALAN CLAYSON

The sessions at 320 East 21st Street made complete sense for Fleetwood Mac, a group that might not have even existed had it not been for the inspiration of the Chicago blues that lived in the building as pungently and as pragmatically as it did in the down-and-out State Street busker, lilting an unaccompanied and never-ending "Hoochie Coochie Man" as if optimistic of sexual congress, possibly on the very pavement.

**Alan Clayson**
English singer-songwriter, author, and music journalist. He gained popularity in the late 1970s as leader of the band Clayson and the Argonauts.

Otis Spann, John McVie

## DANNY KIRWAN, OBITUARY

Fleetwood said, "Danny worked out great from the start. His playing was always very melodic and tuneful, with lots of bent notes and vibrato. Danny's style of playing complemented Peter's perfectly because he was already a disciple. His sense of melody on rhythm guitar really drew Peter out, allowing him to write songs in a different style. Playing live, he was a madman." Fleetwood Mac biographer Leah Furman said Kirwan, "provided a perfect sounding board for Peter's ideas, added stylistic texture, and moved Fleetwood Mac away from pure blues."

Danny Kirwan, Peter Green, Otis Spann, John McVie

## JOE BONAMASSA

Peter Green, in the pantheon of great British and non-British guitarists alike, deserved a seat at the table with Beck, Page, and Clapton. His influence and music stand the test of time. His underrated voice and extraordinary ability to communicate the blues in the simplest sense were his greatest strengths. Having the opportunity to play Peter's Les Paul at Royal Albert Hall a few years back was an honor of the highest order. It was because of Peter and the gang of about a dozen players that discovered that the Sunburst Les Paul was the ideal rock-and-roll delivery vehicle that it has spurred countless copies and has gone down as legend. It will always be legendary, and so will the music. Fifty-plus years on, and we are still chasing something that Peter made look effortless.

**Joe Bonamassa**
American blues-rock guitarist, singer, and songwriter

Peter Green, John McVie

Peter Green, Danny Kirwan, Otis Spann, John McVie

# PAUL HAMER

It was a Sunday, I think. My youngest son had to go to the local library for a school paper. As he searched for his books, I decided to wander the library's art gallery. It was opening day for a photography exhibition, and a group of people had surrounded the artist. They were discussing his work. I looked at the photographs and stopped, mesmerized by one. Where had I seen it before? Why would I have seen it before? It was a photo of a Black man wearing sunglasses, indoors. As the crowd surrounding the artist dispersed, I approached the photographer and asked where he had taken the picture. "Chess Records," he said. "I was a *Newsweek* photographer and also the house photographer at Chess."

That was my introduction to Jeff Lowenthal, the kindest, most humble chronicler of the 1960s. I grew up in the Chicago suburbs. As a kid knocked out by music, I often made my way to Chicago's music row on the weekends. At that time, musical instrument stores lined both sides of Wabash Street under the El tracks. Kroch's and Bretano's bookstore and Rose Records were my favorite haunts. Rose Records had a vast selection, and the pricing was slightly better than my local record store in the suburbs. They stocked all the new releases and had hundreds of old records. It was there that I discovered *Fleetwood Mac in Chicago*, a two-record set. Two-record sets were uncommon

then. Sets were twice as much money as single records, so for kids on limited budgets, you had to choose carefully. And what a record for the money. I was in awe of the cover. There were color and black-and-white photos scattered all over the outside and the inside centerfold. Lots of them. I could see the instruments my heroes were playing. I could see the amps they were using. In the 1960s, this was a revelation and an inspiration. There is one tiny black-and-white photograph on the inside cover that I could not stop admiring. It's a perfectly framed wide-angle shot of Peter Green holding his guitar. This photo stayed with me over the years. Little did I know how these people and this record would crisscross my life, intersecting at the oddest moments.

I started building guitars in 1974. People often ask me why I began. I was fed up with the quality of the guitars the large corporations were manufacturing, and with the bravado of youth on my side, I decided to see if I could do it myself. Amazingly, people started buying my guitars right away, and within a few years I was selling Hamer guitars all over the world. My company came to the attention of *Rolling Stone* magazine. During the interview, I mentioned how I always wanted to have my guitars emulate Peter Green's and Danny Kirwan's distinctive sound. Later that year, I found myself in London at Rod Argent's music store. The manager, Howard Brain, had invited me to do a Saturday morning in-store visit

John McVie, Peter Green, Danny Kirwan

Peter Green

Jeremy Spencer, Mick Fleetwood, Mike Vernon, Peter Green

to demonstrate my guitars. I was talking to a group of people when one of them turned and walked out of the store. Howard came over to me and said, "Do you know who that was? That was Danny Kirwan!" I asked if someone would ask him to come back in. You can imagine I had a million questions for him. When Danny came back in, he wasn't too interested in talking, so I asked him to play the guitar I had out. He declined, but I got the opportunity to tell him what an inspiration he had been to me, and how the guitar I was holding was a multiyear effort to get that Fleetwood Mac sound.

Meanwhile, the new version of Fleetwood Mac was very successful and touring all over the world. My brother John caught up with them at a show in Chicago. John brought some basses to show John McVie, and John took a liking to a solid-mahogany Hamer Cruisebass. You can see videos of him playing it live.

During the 1980s, I had the pleasure of building guitars for Gary Moore. Gary visited the Hamer factory, and we were in my office playing different guitars through a small amp. I had heard that he

had Peter's guitar, so I got up the courage to ask him if he had brought it. "Yeah, I did," he said. "Want to play it?" He had it in the car out in the parking lot. He went out and brought it back in. Apparently, it rarely left his side. We spent the rest of the afternoon swapping licks on Peter's guitar, with Gary showing me how Peter approached playing. He gave me some tips on how Danny Kirwan played "Jigsaw Puzzle Blues." It was magical. Here I was, playing the guitar, the guitar that I had admired through Jeff Lowenthal's photographs so many years before. The photos in this book are from January 4, 1969. A little more than a year later, Peter ended his time with Fleetwood Mac. In the annals of music, it may be one of the shortest careers ever. However, it is also one of the most influential. Peter's voice and his playing carry on to this day, captivating musicians all over the world. Thankfully for us, Jeff's photos document this influential time in music.

**Paul Hamer**
Founder, Hamer Guitars

John McVie, Honeyboy Edwards, Peter Green

## Lyle Workman

Clapton was legendary from ubiquitous radio play in the 1960s and 1970s, but when I discovered Peter Green I couldn't believe he wasn't as well known, because his playing was every bit as sensational and groundbreaking.

**Lyle Workman**
American guitarist, composer, session and touring musician, music producer

Danny Kirwan, John McVie, Otis Spann, Peter Green

John McVie, Peter Green, Willie Dixon

## TONY STEVENS

Savoy Brown did a few shows with Peter's Fleetwood Mac. Before I joined Savoy, I went for an audition for a guitarist that the Mac were sponsoring. His name was Danny Kirwan. I got the job but was told later that Danny had joined Fleetwood Mac. I remember—I think it was Canada, maybe a college in America—that Savoy and Fleetwood had done a show together, and afterward I sat with Peter, jamming some blues, and started playing "Albatross," one of my favorite songs.

**Tony Stevens**
Bassist, Savoy Brown and Foghat

Danny Kirwan, John McVie, Peter Green, Stu Black

Peter Green

## AYNSLEY DUNBAR, INTERVIEW

**Robert Schaffner**: You wrote a song with Peter called "Rubber Duck"?

**Aynsley Dunbar**: Oh wow! Remembering "Rubber Duck." Boy, that goes back a ways. That was only one of those things we just threw together, basically—it was a drum solo. One of those things we just came up with a riff and put it together and then played the riff, then a drum solo. It's one of those things that just happened.

**RS**: Do you recall working with him?

**AD**: Yes, well, my first thought that came to mind when I first heard what you guys you were doing was, when I got the offer from John Mayall, he sort of came on the phone . . . I had just went down to . . . Soho and sat in with Alexis Korner. And I wasn't really happy with what happened. So we went back to Alexis's house, and he told me this was the best thing that I could ever to do with him, and I went back home depleted! . . . 'cause I had a good gig. . . . Next thing, I got a call from John Mayall. He said, by the way, I saw you playing last night, so I would be interested if you'd be hearing and seeing the band and like to play with them? I looked at my wife and said who the heck is John Mayall? So she said: " I think he's a country western guy." Oh no!! So, okay, I'll go down there and see them. Got there and went into the balcony, the first band finishes, and John comes on stage; Peter Green opened up . . . and soon as he opened up and started playing guitar, I have to play with him. It was just one of those things. He played with so much feeling! He pretty much well wiped me out—right there! I had been playing pop music with the Mojos up to that point; a few blues and all the regular rock-and-roll stuff that was happening in England back then. That was my real first taste of blues, and I just fell over backward. I had never felt so much that come off and out of a guitar. As soon as I played with Peter, it was

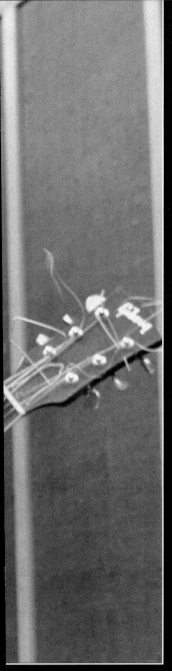

Danny Kirwan, Peter
Green, John McVie

Mick Fleetwood, Mike
Vernon, Peter Green,
John McVie

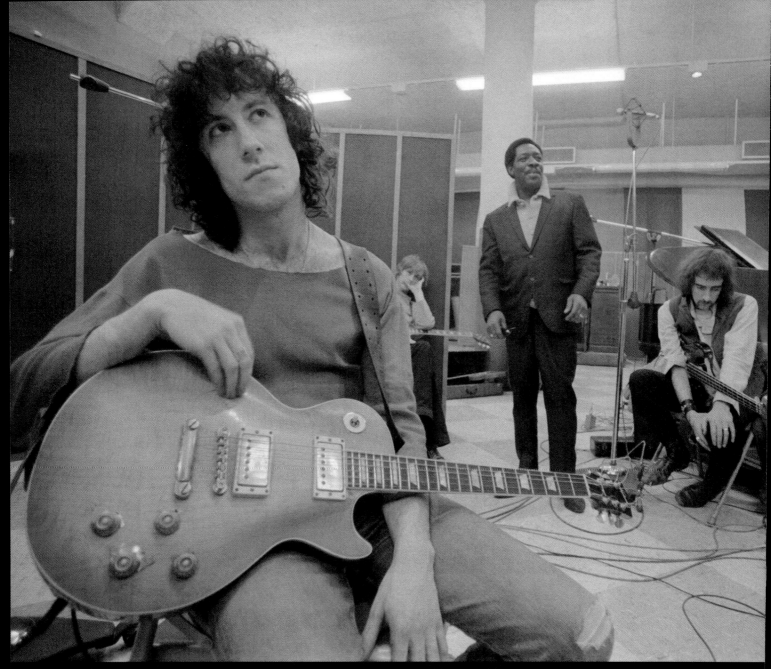

Peter Green, Danny Kirwan, Otis Spann, John McVie

like . . . he was my "mark" as a guitarist of who I could play with . . . and who really didn't turn me about. . . . I have played with some of the greatest guitarists to be named . . . that tend to go home every night to make sure they get the solo perfectly right. So with a band it was boring as hell, 'cause all you hear is the same guitar solo, but with Peter every night it was a different solo. That's what I loved about the band!

**RS**: I have heard this from many; people would ask Peter after a concert, "How did you play such and such?" Peter would say, "I don't know what you mean; I just play what I feel."

**AD**: Exactly! I used to play what I felt too. I was only with the band for about six months. I didn't want to play that old blues feel. So I just moved on. You play with the same band and play the same thing, then they tell you they want you to play just like the record . . . so you turn that down and end up losing millions of dollars. Because your own internal healing

. . . you just cannot be put down to playing the same thing every night. I was just amazed at that. As the business moved on, it became corporate rock. It wasn't the music being played on stage . . . it was the lights and the sound guy . . . they would have to know everything that's happening, so it had to be the same thing every night, because they couldn't adapt.

**Aynsley Dunbar**

English drummer. He has worked with John Mayall, Frank Zappa, Jeff Beck, Journey, Jefferson Starship, Nils Lofgren, Eric Burdon, Shuggie Otis, Ian Hunter, Lou Reed, David Bowie, Mick Ronson, Whitesnake, Pat Travers, Sammy Hagar, Michael Schenker, UFO, Michael Chapman, Jake E. Lee, Leslie West, Kathi McDonald, Keith Emerson, Mike Onesko, Herbie Mann, and Flo & Eddie. Dunbar was inducted into the Rock and Roll Hall of Fame as a member of Journey in 2017

Peter Green, John McVie, Mick Fleetwood, Danny Kirwan

## DEA MATRONA

The first riff I learnt on the guitar was "Oh Well" after I discovered a clip of Fleetwood Mac playing it live on YouTube. I was immediately enchanted by the dynamic riff of the song and the incredible voice and guitar playing of Peter Green; it set off a spark with me, and I made it my mission to start playing electric guitar. Peter's ability to make the guitar an emotional force is why he is one of the greats; whether it's the iconic solo on "Black Magic Woman" or his soulful vocals at the end of "The Green Manalishi," he truly is a unique talent that has inspired so many people.

**Orláith Forsythe**
Guitars/vocals

Before Dea Matrona was formed, myself and Orláith used to jam together after school. We both were getting into Fleetwood Mac, and "Oh Well" was one of the tracks that we started playing together because we loved the intertwining guitar lines of Danny Kirwan and Peter Green. We decided to bring it into our set, as it represents the beginnings of our band, jamming songs together that we all love to play.

**Mollie McGinn**
Guitars/vocals. Dea Matrona are a trio from Ireland, Carryduff and Dundrum.

Peter Green, Danny Kirwan, John McVie

Peter Green

## CHRIS SPEDDING

I remember being in the studio with Peter Green one time only. It was a session for Memphis Slim, and the producer was Philippe Rault. I remember feeling lucky I was in such exalted company. Can't remember much else!

**Chris Spedding**
Singer, guitarist, songwriter, multi-instrumentalist, composer, and record producer

## JON TIVEN

When Fleetwood Mac journeyed to Chicago and recorded at the famed Chess Studios, they weren't doing it to prove their authenticity. B.B. King had already sung the praises of Peter Green in interviews, and once you get the nod from Riley you're in an exclusive club. And yes, both the Yardbirds and the Rolling Stones had recorded in Chess Studios, but they were using only the facility, not the musicians. I'm sure there was some special mojo in that room, but the magic of the recordings there lies with the musicians and singers—at least as much as with the engineers, microphones, and baffles. They were mixing it up with Willie Dixon, Otis Spann, Shakey Horton, Buddy Guy—also J. T. Brown, Honeyboy Edwards, and S. P. Leary—cutting their own songs as well as their new friends' material. Jeremy Spencer was living out his Elmore James fantasies, Danny Kirwan was blossoming as a singer and writer, and John McVie and Mick Fleetwood would jump in and out of the picture. Peter Green was soaking it all in and spitting it back out again as only he could, a classic moment in the progression of blues music.

My encounter with Peter Green was much later, late nineties in New York City. He was playing with an outfit directed by a fellow named Nigel, who was as much Green's minder as his guitarist. There were quite a few musicians and fans who turned out to see and meet him, and I was a little

John McVie, Shakey Horton, Peter Green

wary of Peter. A very good friend of mine who had been a special guest on some of Green's comeback shows in the UK told me he had to drop out because Peter's treatment of people, particularly Cozy Powell (his drummer), was appalling and left him feeling poorly after the shows. I certainly didn't want to experience the back of Peter Green's hand, so I introduced myself as having recently produced records by Wilson Pickett and B.B. King (which was true). His eyes perked up, he looked straight at me, and he said, "You must be very good." My friend who accompanied me to the show, Jol Dantzig, had designed the ax Peter currently played (the "Miller" guitar), so Peter exhibited more

interest in talking with the two of us than anybody else. We hung with him for a while before the show, and none of his temper flares exhibited themselves in our presence, He was actually quite nice. Peter was signing albums for the fans, and most of them he signed Peter Greenbaum, but mine he signed Peter Green. That's my take on Fleetwood Mac in Chicago and my interaction with the man most responsible for it, Enjoy the music.

**Jon Tiven**
American composer, guitarist, record producer, and music journalist

Peter Green, John McVie

Mike Vernon, Peter Green, Mick Fleetwood, Jeremy Spencer, Buddy Guy

John McVie, Peter Green

Peter Green, Danny Kirwan

## JOL DANTZIG

Jeff Lowenthal's book is a visual time capsule—a gift to lovers of American music and fans of Fleetwood Mac. Having been formed in London only a year before, it wasn't surprising that Lowenthal wasn't familiar with the band when he arrived at Chicago's Chess studio on January 4, 1969, to photograph the recording sessions that became *Fleetwood Mac in Chicago*. Yet, he perfectly captured the essence of those brief sessions—a summit between the venerable blues masters of Chicago and the young disciples from overseas.

Four days earlier I had celebrated the new year at the Kinetic Playground, a music venue on Chicago's North side. By the time Muddy Waters and the Byrds had finished their sets and midnight had come and gone, I was starting to get sleepy. But then Fleetwood Mac launched into their first number—a stunning blues shuffle that arrived with the power and cadence of a locomotive pulling out of a station, and I was wide awake and wide eyed. The three-guitar attack of Peter Green, Jeremy Spencer, and the young Danny Kirwan,

combined with the rock-solid underpinnings of bassist John McVie and drummer Mick Fleetwood, was just the way to start off 1969. It was something I've never forgotten.

Although Fleetwood Mac was revered in their native England, relatively few listeners in America understood their importance to the growing blues movement at the time. One could easily argue that their pilgrimage to Chicago's Chess studios was a pivotal moment in the arc not only of Fleetwood Mac's career, but the course of modern electric blues. If there was any doubt in the minds of the local Chicago musicians who were invited to perform with these somewhat unknown, young, British musicians, it soon evaporated once the session was underway. And, like a fly on the wall, Jeff Lowenthal and his camera were there to record everything as it unfolded. I'm grateful that these images can finally put us right in the studio with him.

**Jol Dantzig**
Artist, businessman, songwriter, designer, guitarist, luthier, author, and one of the founders of Hamer Guitars

Peter Green, Danny Kirwan

Peter Green, John McVie

Mike Vernon, Peter Green, Honeyboy Edwards, Buddy Guy, Stu Black, Jeremy Spencer, Willie Dixon, Shakey Horton

Danny Kirwan

## STEVE SUMMERS

Peter Green. Oh, well. What should I say? My favorite electric guitarists are the ones who put very little between the touch of their fingers on the strings, their picking, and what comes out of the amp; who rely on magnets and steel, some wires and tubes and electronic bits in a circuit to produce the glorious sound the speakers put out. The truly special ones are the few who put very little between their heart and soul, and the unmistakable sounds and melodies they produce via direct connection to the infinite. Peter

Green was one of those otherworldly beings. He said he talked to God, and I believe he did. God spoke through him. The color of his sound is what I see when I think of the ideal guitar tone. His vibrato is what I feel when a note touches my heart. When he sang, his voice always rang true. Peter suffered mightily for the gifts he was given. His music is imbued with the innocent sadness and everlasting beauty of a tortured soul who played what he felt.

**Steve "Smooth" Summers**
Artist, musician, songwriter, EIEIO, Empire of Fun

Buddy Guy, Mike Vernon, Peter Green, Stu Black, Willie Dixon

## WALTER TROUT, INTERVIEW

**Walter Trout**: I am actually a Danny Kirwan fan too. A lot of the great stuff on their early Fleetwood Mac albums that Peter got credit for was actually Danny. He was just incredible.

**Robert Schaffner**: My opinion, Danny had the best vibrato of any guitarist.

**WT**: YES! That is funny you say that—I watched a video of Danny Kirwan and Peter Green rehearsing in someone's living room . . . on the song "One Sunny Day" . . . yeah, and you hear—they don't even have amplifiers plugged in—and you hear Danny playing the high parts of the song . . . and that vibrato when he's playing the high part along with doubling the vocal—that vibrato is fucking incredible! So I agree, man! He is not given the credit he deserves. That is my thought on that guy.

**RS**: There are some people I know who got to play Peter's 1959 Les Paul when Gary Moore owned it, and they all said none of them sounded like Peter when they played that guitar.

**WT**: No, not even Gary Moore didn't sound like Peter Green when he played that guitar. And now Kirk Hammett owns it now, and he certainly doesn't sound like Peter Green . . . [giggles]

**RS**: On your new LP, the song "Ordinary Madness," your solo begins on the bass strings and you work around from there, much like Peter did on some of his solos . . .

**WT**; Thank you; thanks, man. I have a theory about solos. A lot of people don't get it. People ask me what is my best solo you have ever heard, and I say the "I Have a Dream" speech by Martin Luther King. He starts off slow, he builds and builds, and he gets to the climax, and at the end, nothing more need be said. And that is what a solo should do.

**RS**: When did you first encounter Peter Green?

**WT**: Well, I first got turned on to Peter Green when he was with Mayall. I was right on that thing, man, the *Beano* album, and I studied it. So you know who succeeded Clapton; it was Peter Green, *A Hard Road* and those albums with Mayall [also referring to the two 1967 live releases from Forty Below Records]; I was just blown away! I have to say when he played with Mayall, I liked his playing better than Clapton's. I don't know what it was, but when I say fire or passion, .the passion he played on those records was just unbelievable. Then I followed him from then on, and when he left Mayall and started his own band, I was right there. I had all their stuff, I studied all their stuff.

**RS**: Peter Green played from his heart.

**WT**: He also—I don't know how to say this without sounding too foo-foo or some bullshit—but Peter's playing has a spiritual aspect to it. It comes from deep in a place, and I actually think

Danny Kirwan, John McVie

it's beyond that place in his heart; there's some-thing happening with that guy, when he was playing that stuff. It's as deep as listening to Miles Davis or Coltrane or something. Even though he's not playing that kind of music, the depth of what he is putting out, sorry . . . I gonna start crying [voice chokes up] . . . it's just beautiful . . . the feeling it gave me, the depth of his in-volvement and commitment of where it's coming from, is a deep space, and sometimes it almost hurts to listen to.

**RS**: Since you're a harp player too, can you make some comments on Peter's playing, and did you ever see him live?

**WT**: Well, he played great harp, but just being me, I wanted to hear him play guitar, ya know. [laughs] . . . When Peter made his comeback in the 1990s, I guess, I did get to meet him. I'm okay with meeting those people, but with Peter Green I didn't know what to say, and he was very quiet and reserved. I did try to talk to him a little, saying I also played with John Mayall, and ya' know, thanks for the inspiration you've given me, and it's great you're back. He kinda looked and smiled, didn't say much; he shook my hand, then I left; I felt uncomfortable. I felt like I was invading his privacy, and he kinda wanted to be left alone; I was in awe! I was just listening to *Fleetwood Mac in Chicago*, which I bought when I was fifteen . . . and another thing he did, he would alternate between having the reverb on his amp on or off, and sometimes in the middle of a solo he would kick the reverb on, and a lot of times he played completely dry without the reverb . . . ya' know, the guy was something else, man. Another thing is those old Fleetwood Mac albums; don't know what it is, if it was Mike Vernon, but the way they're recorded and mixed it's awesome; it's like you're in the room with the band. The sound of those records is like nothing else, man, so rare and in your face and so true to what that band was doing. They are just great sounding records.

**Walter Trout**
American blues guitarist, singer and songwriter, Canned Heat, John Mayall, solo

Danny Kirwan

Peter Green, Danny
Kirwan, John McVie

Danny Kirwan

Shakey Horton, Danny Kirwan

Mick Fleetwood

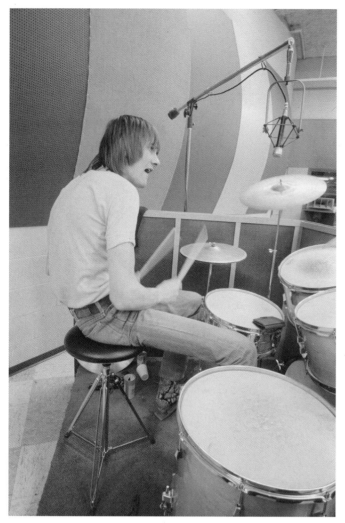

Mick Fleetwood

Peter Green

## MIKE HOFFMAN

At this flickering beginning of what would become a career and lifetime in music, I was essentially a drummer—but my most valuable asset was my ability to sing and harmonize. This was a sure ticket into a band; however, there was already a drummer with a kit—I had no kit—so I picked up the guitar to survive! I actually was playing professionally as I was learning to play; it sped up the learning process with frightening intensity.

Peter Green's tone and technique was so clear, original, and simple that it always reached the target and inspired imitation—I just tried to play like him. With his passing recently, it really transported me back to that time in 1970, the beginning, when I heard him for the first time . . . sweet, innocent inspiration. Thank you, Peter Green.

**Mike Hoffman**, RIP
Recording artist, producer at RCA, Demon, Frontier, Warner Bros., Fox, Almo Sounds / Geffen
www.mikehoffman.net

Otis Spann

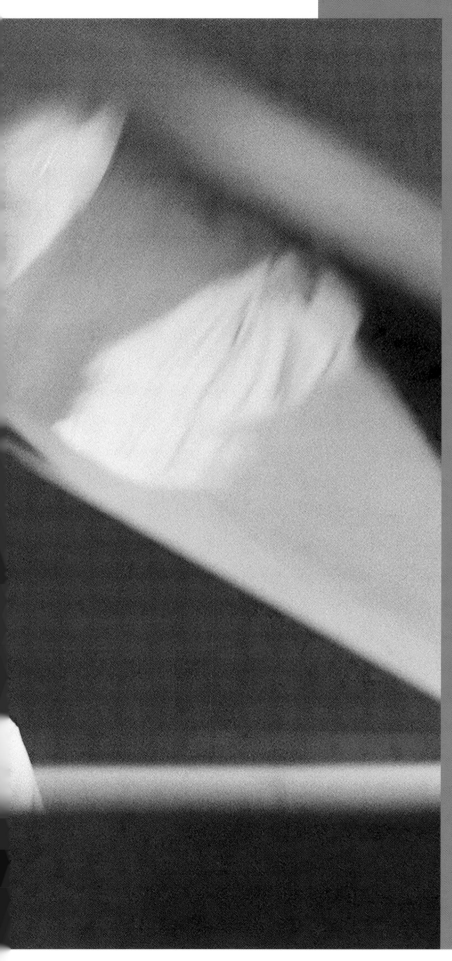

# MICHAEL FREEMAN

The mid- to late 1960s in the UK saw the emergence of a great many electric blues bands, some spearheaded by John Mayall's lineups and subsequent alumni of his Bluesbreakers, and in addition to bands such as Savoy Brown and Chicken Shack, to name but a few.

Peter Green's Fleetwood Mac are undoubtedly one of the most memorable bands of that time period, and their first two albums and this double album, documenting the Chicago sessions at Chess Studios and released in 1969 on Mike Vernon's Blue Horizon label, were very much a part of album collections in the UK.

Peter Green's emotional and economical style on guitar was refreshing, and in great contrast to the higher-octane styles of some contemporaries. His phrasing was careful but powerful. He was also a generous player and band leader, as witnessed by the space he gave Danny Kirwan both on record and on stage.

Peter's generosity also extended to the fans of Fleetwood Mac, with whom he would willingly engage in sometimes long and detailed conversation after a gig. I enjoyed one of those conversations at a college gig in London, but I gather those after-gig extensions were held much to the annoyance of the other band members, who just wanted to leave!

In addition to the depth of his style both live and on record, his accessibility to fans absolutely endeared him to those who had the chance to meet him on those occasions.

The previews of Jeff Lowenthal's images that I have seen are stunning, and this book will be a superb and essential addition to the collections of Peter Green's Fleetwood Mac fans and serious blues lovers alike. This unique collection gives a visual rendering of the bridge that connected the British blues musicians and the American blues masters who were their mentors and heroes, in a rare studio setting.

**Michael Freeman**
Grammy and Blues Music Award–winning producer, recipient of the Keeping the Blues Alive (KBA) award

Buddy Guy, Mike Vernon

Peter Green, John McVie

Peter Green, John McVie, Danny Kirwan

Otis Spann

Shakey Horton, Danny Kirwan

# CURTIS MEISSNER

As an eighteen-year-old guitarist back in the early 1970s, I was heavily influenced by the three great British blues guitarists I had heard playing with John Mayall's Bluesbreakers: Eric Clapton, Peter Green, and Mick Taylor. I learned everything I could about their phrasing, tone, and technique. There was one thing that really stunned me—that incredible sound that Peter Green was able to get out of his Sunburst Les Paul. I owned a 1959 Les Paul at the time, but I just couldn't figure out what he was doing. The attack, vibrato, and phrasing were beautiful, but his tone was magical. I bought every recording I could find of Peter's work with Fleetwood Mac, and solo releases, and spent hours learning every lick I could. Working as a technician at Hamer Guitars for twenty years, I spent many hours in the development of numerous guitar models, always testing electronics, pickups, and various woods in my personal quest to emulate that tone I had heard from Peter Green years earlier. I was never able to do it, since I realized it was all Peter. He was a true genius, one in a million.

**Curtis Meissner**
Guitarist, luthier at Hamer Guitars, Washburn

Danny Kirwan, John McVie, Peter Green, Stu Black

Shakey Horton, Buddy Guy, Mike Vernon, Peter Green

Mike Vernon, Peter Green, T. J. Leary, Mick Fleetwood, Jeremy Spencer, Willie Dixon, Buddy Guy

Danny Kirwan, Peter Green, John McVie, Otis Spann

Peter Green, John McVie

## GARY GAND

My family folk trio, the Gand Family Singers, was in San Francisco to play several shows at the Berkeley Folk Festival the week of July 4, 1968.

Determined to go to the Fillmore West, I read a short bit in *Rolling Stone* about Peter Green's new post-Mayall band, Fleetwood Mac. Low and behold, they were playing that night at the Fillmore on a bill with the Paul Butterfield Blues Band (Bill Graham's favorite) and an unknown act called Ten Years After.

I got my dad to drive me to what was the new location of the Fillmore West, and waited in line to get in. Many decades later, there was a photo of the Fillmore West published, and there I am standing in line!

At the time, the band was Peter and Jeremy Spencer only. They spent the evening playing blues covers, going back and forth from Jeremy's classic Chicago-style slide and Peter's more up-tempo B.B. King outings. All good, but traditional, by my standards.

**Gary Gand**
Guitarist, Gand Band

Jeremy Spencer, Buddy Guy

## BUDDY GUY, INTERVIEW

**Robert Schaffner**: Hi Buddy, nice to meet you over the phone.

**Buddy Guy**: Hi, Bob; how are you?

**RS**: [explained about the book] By the way, you also were wearing some kick-ass boots!

**BG**: Haha . . . well, that goes way back there, ya know . . . I was being interviewed yesterday, and I remember all those guys coming into Chess; come in and jam with us. I first went to England in 1965, before any of us got famous. And there was Jeff Beck, Eric Clapton, and Jimmy Page, and they didn't know the blues could be played on a Strat, and we just cracked up on that, man. And we still laugh about it.

**RS**: We have photos of you playing a Strat, wearing a British cap and those mean boots.

**BG**: Yeah, yeah; man, those guys really helped not just Buddy Guy . . . but when the British guys started playing the hard-core blues of, you know, Robert Johnson and all those blues guys, who lots of Americans didn't recognize, and they came in here and played that type of music. It woke up American to the blues of Muddy Waters, Howlin' Wolf, and people like that.

**RS**: Did you recall playing with Peter Green, Danny Kirwan, and Jeremy Spencer?

**BG**: Yeah! Yeah! You know . . . actually, maybe I shouldn't say a thing about Peter Green, but this must have been thirty to forty years ago, when he did a concert in Chicago and I went to see him and asked him if he remembered me at those sessions, and he said, "No." [laughter]

**RS**: [I recall a story to Buddy that Peter didn't recall Mick Taylor either during that same time period.]

Buddy Guy, Mike Vernon,
Shakey Horton, Peter Green

Buddy Guy

Jeremy Spencer, Buddy Guy

**BG**: Wow! I know when you get flashbacks. You know when you get to an age; I got a birthday next month, and I will be eighty-five years old, and I began to feel it. I saw B.B. right before he passed, and he was forgetting lyrics and I am saying, like, what's going on? But now . . . I'll tell ya, me and the late Tyrone Davis would look at a song once and memorize it and throw the paper away. Now I have to go to bed with the song, and I still can't remember it!

**RS**: And B.B. King once said Peter Green was one of the only guys that made him sweat!

**BG**: Yeah, those guys were great! They woke up America about the blues, more than America had been awakened before. I hope I am not changing what we are talking about . . . think it was around 1964 or so, I was doing a song in the studio, and all of a sudden in the session, out steps these guys with high boots on and long, long, hair, and I started to cursing, Who is this? It was the Rolling Stones. Muddy Waters had helped them bring their instruments up, and they were trying to do a demo for Chess Records.

**RS**: Buddy, can you say a comment about Peter Green's or Danny Kirwan's playing?

**BG**: Oh, man, those guys were so good! And all I can do is thank them for what they did! Man, you heard things like the British are coming, the British are coming, and when they started playing the blues, man, with those big amps up. Jimi Hendrix had to go to England to get recognized, and the British just said, "I don't care how you play it, just bring it on!" America was saying, "What's that?" They were saying they were not ready for that. We got at Chess Records people like Howlin' Wolf, Muddy Waters, Sonny Boy, Jimmy Rogers, Willie Dixon; guess they figured that's enough. But when the British started playing the blues, Chess called and got Willie Dixon, said go to Buddy Guy's house and get him and bring him here. Because they used to criticize me for turning that amp up before I knew anything about British guys playing the blues. I was doing what Guitar Slim had did down in Louisiana; kinda turned the amplifier up while Ray Charles was making arrangements for him.

Buddy Guy, Peter Green, Honeyboy Edwards

**RS**: Do you remember the atmosphere around Chess?

**BG**: If I heard a guy who heard somebody who was playing something joyful to my ears, I'm saying bring 'em on! I can learn something from them. I wanted to hear what they were doing.

**RS**: So you all learned from each other?

**BG**: Oh yeah, yeah; that's my lesson. Through my whole career listening to other people, didn't care if they were old or young, I wanted to hear what they were doing. If you had interviewed me forty years ago, I was like a tape recorder; I hadn't forgotten nothin'. But those brains ain't what they used to be.

**RS**: Peter Green would play the same songs, but the solos were always a little different each night.

**BG**: Right. You know they used to have in Chicago, if you had a little 45 come out, the disc jockey would go to clubs and spin records. If you had a record out, they would invite you to come out and lip-sync. I'd say, man, I can even play along with my own records!

**RS**: But isn't that what blues is all about; it's only good for that moment in time, right?

**BG**: Yes! You know, when I go play blues now and playing in front of an audience, I forget about myself. If I'm playing a song and I see I got you going my way, I'd play that three–four-minute song for ten minutes, twenty minutes, 'cause I could do that, and if I got you in my hand, I am here to let you know who I am and how I'm enjoying you, as much as you are enjoying me.

**RS**: That's what the blues is about, right? It's played from your heart. Right, Buddy?

**BG**: That's right! That's so correct!

**RS**: And that is what is said about Peter Green; he played from his heart.

**BG**: Oh, yeah, all of them did; B.B. did too. Man, him, Jeff Beck, and all those British guys, we need to give them credit.

### George "Buddy" Guy

American blues guitarist and singer. He is an exponent of Chicago blues and has influenced guitarists including Eric Clapton, Jimi Hendrix, Jimmy Page, Keith Richards, Stevie Ray Vaughan, and Jeff Beck.

Jeremy Spencer, Buddy Guy

Jeremy Spencer, Buddy Guy

Mike Vernon, Peter Green, Mick Fleetwood

## ANDY ELLIS

Hearing "The Supernatural" for the first time changed my entire approach to playing lead guitar. In 1967, when John Mayall & the Bluesbreakers released *A Hard Road*, I was living in Germany, playing in a band called the Abstracts. The moment our drummer scored a copy of the album, we eagerly convened a listening session. We were digging the songs and sound—much bluesier than our normal diet of the Who, Kinks, and Pretty Things—but when we reached side 2, track 4, Peter Green blew my fifteen-year-old mind. I'd heard feedback before—I'd even tinkered with it myself as a way to

add drama to the end of a song, à la Pete Townshend—but I'd never conceived of using controlled feedback as an electric bow. Each of Green's keening, ten-second notes gave me goose bumps. I was also captivated by how he used his pick: rather than simply pluck the strings with a clean attack, as I'd been taught, he angled it to add a subtle rasping sound that gave his phrases a vocal quality. I thought, "*This* is how I want to play guitar!" Decades later, that's still true.

**Andy Ellis**
Veteran guitar journalist and former senior editor at *Guitar Player* and *Premier Guitar*

Danny Kirwan, Peter Green

Danny Kirwan

# CHRIS HERMAN

### DANNY KIRWAN

I keep a clearing in my mind for the people I admire: the Bluesbreakers . . . or unique clearings for each. Danny Kirwan occupies one of those clearings. There's something about him that reminds me of that scene in *Tron* where the players discover a spring of pure energy and drink from it to recharge themselves. Danny Kirwan doesn't have the same legendary status as Peter Green, but maybe that's because the persons who would be his audience couldn't find him . . . couldn't navigate across the wilderness of British blues to find him.

What a strange combination of abilities and aptitudes: a voice like a choirboy's, a thrilling energetic vibrato as a guitarist, a gift for genre-spanning compositions as rollicking as "One Sunny Day"; as antique, inventive, and virtuosic as "Jigsaw Puzzle Blues"; and as light and exhilarating as "Earl Gray." It's amazing he lived as long as he did, considering that his is the kind of being that God calls back to heaven early . . . but while he lived, he was an angel here on earth.

**Chris Herman**
Guitarist, friend of the memory of Fleetwood Mac

Danny Kirwan

Peter Green, Otis Spann, Danny Kirwan, John McVie

## MARTIN BARRE

I first met Peter Green in early 1969. I had just joined Jethro Tull and was still in a whirlwind of new music and a completely different environment. I wasn't finding it easy, and my nerves were in overdrive.

Our bass player, Glen Cornick, was a good friend of the members of Fleetwood Mac and asked me if I would like to meet Peter. We went to see him at his parents' house, where he lived at the time, and he welcomed us both to tea and chat!

I remember we sat on his bed (it was a small house!) in his room, and me and Peter played guitars with Glen on bass. I don't remember what we played, but I know he was so encouraging and positive with his help.

The fact that he was a very gentle and good person put me so much at ease in his company, and remembering he was probably the most important guitarist in the UK at that time! He seemed at odds with the mainstream "big ego" rock stars of the day, but his amazing voice and playing transcended all around him.

He was truly a special person, and our paths would cross occasionally on the road, but never as much as I wished.

His phrasing, invention, and sound will stand out forever in the history of the blues guitar.

**Martin Barre**
English guitarist, lead guitarist of British rock band Jethro Tull

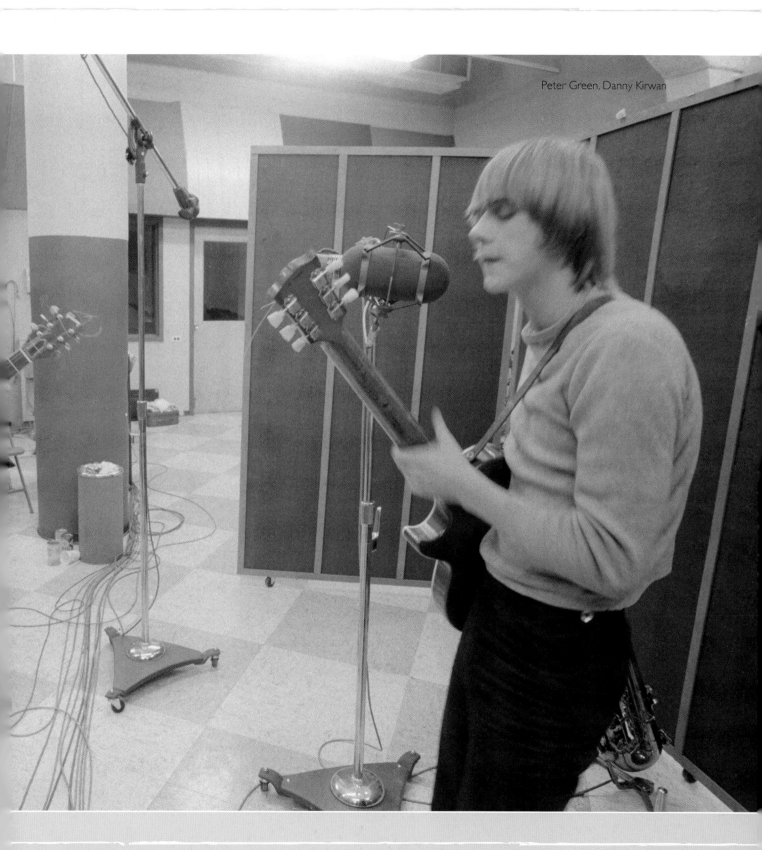

Peter Green, Danny Kirwan

Jeremy Spencer, Willie Dixon

## ANDY GALLAGHER

It's August 13, 1994. I'm fourteen years old, and I've stayed up all night listening to the live BBC coverage of Woodstock '94. I had already heard so many great bands, including Jackyl, Violent Femmes, Nine Inch Nails, and Metallica, to name but a few, and it's now 5:00 or 6:00 a.m. (UK time), and my favorite band Aerosmith is ripping it up onstage. I'm loving every second of it, then Steven Tyler announces Joe Perry is gonna sing a couple of songs. The next thing is Joe starts playing this song called "Stop Messin' Around." My jaw hit the floor, I was completely blown away.

I'd never heard this song before. It obviously sounded like Aerosmith, but it didn't! I eventually found out it was an old Peter Green–era Fleetwood Mac song. I then visited every record store in my area I could. Eventually tracked down and bought *Mr. Wonderful* and *Then Play On* and got hooked on the Peter Green Fleetwood Mac sound.

I couldn't believe these albums were over twenty-five years old already, but man, they were filled with life, fun, and great guitar work. So much so my wife bought me a Les Paul guitar for my fortieth birthday, and the one and only thing I immediately did was mod the neck pickup to be the Peter Green mod.

Earlier this year I was very pleased to read that Kirk Hammett of Metallica now has Green's guitar and is showing it much love. It goes to show it doesn't matter what genre you play; Peter Green has and always will be very influential. Every generation seems to pass on his brilliance, musicality, and passion. Long may that continue. Peace, hugs, and much respect.

**Andy Gallagher**
American singer/songwriter/musician from band formed in Scotland, Overhaul
overhaulmusic.com

Danny Kirwan, Peter Green, Otis Spann, John McVie

Otis Spann

Shakey Horton, Buddy Guy, Mike Vernon, Peter Green

# ROGER C. REALE

I was on to John Mayall immediately, so following Peter was a no-brainer. So when *A Hard Road* was released, songs like "The Supernatural" struck me immediately with its atmospherics and tone. And this approach eventually carried through the several instrumentals right up to *Then Play On*. But it was the first LP, the "Dustbin" cover, that cemented my appreciation for Peter's talent. Here was a true interpreter, rather than another slavish copyist, presenting something new and fresh in its deceiving simplicity of attack. Also, anything with Mike Vernon's name on it got my immediate attention anyway.

With the addition of Danny Kirwan, the musical palette expanded and you have great interplay, as well as great songs, such as "One Sunny Day, Coming Your Way" and many others. Danny had a sensitivity that was a perfect match for Peter.

The Chicago set, with legends such as Willie Dixon, Otis Spann, Buddy Guy (who actually would later record a Reale/Tiven song titled Midnight Train), et al., was not so much a validation of the band, for me, as much as another outpouring of creativity, sort of an homage to the music they loved.

While the Chicago sessions certainly stamped their style, it was clearly not the complete picture of what this band was. However, it remains a fitting document of some of the best tracks of British blues.

**Roger C. Reale**
Grammy and W. C. Handy bassist/composer–nominated singer/songwriter

Mike Vernon, Peter Green, John McVie

Mike Vernon, Peter Green, Mick Fleetwood, Jeremy Spencer, Buddy Guy

# GREG PLATZER

Two people changed guitar permanently in the late 1960s: Jimi Hendrix and Peter Green. Hendrix took it to outer space, and Peter Green took it internally to his soul. His ability to play things that we had already heard, but with a fresh and beautiful expression, had a huge effect on so many guitarists . . . no toys needed. Honesty, curiosity, and beauty expressed with two hands and a one huge heart. He gave us all that he could.

**Greg Platzer**
Luthier/guitarist

## RICK NIELSEN

My favorite lineup of Fleetwood Mac:

With the three guitars and three great guitarists, Peter Green, Danny Kirwan, and Jeremy Spencer, Mick Fleetwood and John McVie making such an amazing, tight, powerful English sound.

Tom [Petersson] and I saw them at "Dewey's," a bar with a second-floor club in Madison, Wisconsin, in 1969.

With blues records, it's hard to know which song is on which album, but the era of that Fleetwood Mac, with Peter Green when they were doing "Oh Well," "Fighting for Madge," and "The Green Manalishi with the Two-Pronged Crown," was the ultimate band. They were so tight: Peter Green, Danny Kirwan, Jeremy Spencer—wow. They were unbelievable. The way they played together was something else—this was the original Fleetwood Mac; before the females got involved, that was the stuff.

But still, I'm really glad for all the millions of listeners around the world that loved *Rumors*, *Tusk*, et al. [RN turns deeply sarcastic]; I'm thrilled for you. It makes me happy. I've never been more happy. But if you missed the "Peter Green" Fleetwood Mac, ouch!!

After Peter Green had left the band, and then Danny and Jeremy too, and on one of the very first Fleetwood Mac tour dates with Stevie Nicks and Buckingham, we opened a show with them in La Crosse, Wisconsin, at the Mary Sawyer Auditorium. It was September 23, 1975. We played and stayed until after their show, and we went to their dressing room to introduce

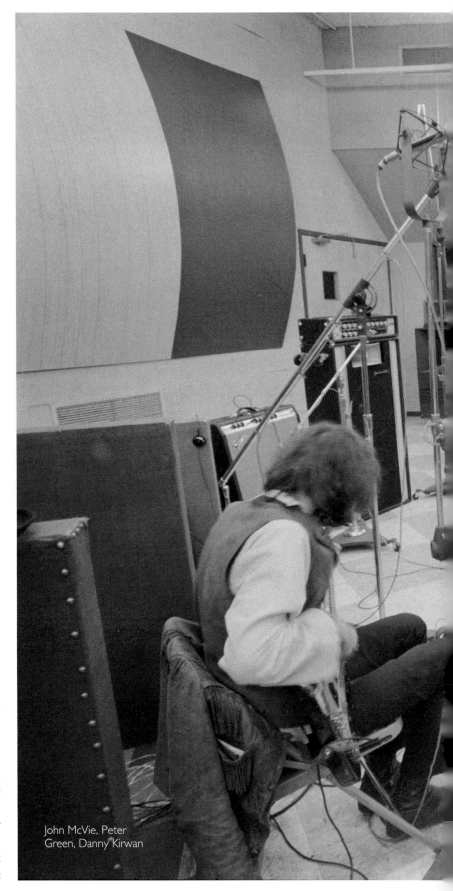

John McVie, Peter Green, Danny Kirwan

Danny Kirwan, Peter Green, Otis Spann, John McVie

ourselves as fans and [to say,] "Thanks for letting us open for you" and "Here are some Cheap Trick shirts for you guys." John McVie stood up and said, "Are you calling my wife a cheap trick? Get out!" and threw us out of the dressing room. Our manager wanted him to apologize to us, as if his wife was a cheap trick. Give me a break. How high was he? Years later in Los Angeles, he apologized and we laughed.

**Rick Nielsen**
Guitarist, Cheap Trick

Peter Green, Mike Vernon, John McVie, Danny Kirwan

Peter Green, John McVie

Jeremy Spencer, Buddy Guy, John McVie, Danny Kirwan

## STEVE MATTHES

Everyone has their favorite guitar player—the one you try to emulate or cop licks off or whatever . . . because it's attainable.

Peter Green is not that for me. Green transcended the role of guitarist to the point where he was more like an actual instrument rather than just a player—a vessel through which miraculous bursts emanated effortlessly, and every sound, tone, or rest was simply perfect. Listening to his playing, you are constantly on the edge of your seat, anxiously awaiting the next note.

**Steve Matthes**
Guitarist and author of *The Ultimate Hamer Guitars: An Illustrated History*

Buddy Guy, Mike Vernon, Peter Green, Willie Dixon

Mick Fleetwood

Mick Fleetwood, Otis Spann

# MICK FLEETWOOD

I think the real reveal of the story of Fleetwood Mac was we were a blues band. We were a bunch of kids playing blues and loving it. And I think what I was thrilled about was we were able to find the photographs—I had some shots, and I thought that was gonna be enough, and then we found a whole slew of extra shots from the sessions at *Blues Jam at Chess* [Fleetwood Mac recorded the album in 1969 with an all-star cast of Chicago blues legends] with Buddy Guy, Otis Spann, Willie Dixon, Shakey Horton, and J. T. Brown, who played saxophone with Elmore James's band, because Elmore had long since passed away. If you listen to early Fleetwood Mac, it's almost exclusively Elmore James material.

Those photographs were in many ways, in terms of the geography, the history of Fleetwood Mac. If you force me to say, "Well, what's the real coup de grace?," I think the fact that we were there, and the story a lot of people don't know about early Peter Green and Fleetwood Mac is that we were

a blues band. And those pictures and finding us at the sessions at Chess Records in Chicago really, really are powerful moments in the story of Fleetwood Mac. And, of course, personally seeing them revealed a whole load of things that one tends to forget. That really was powerful to me, very powerful.

January 1969, we were in Chicago. Mike Vernon found out Chess Records was going to close down its fabled studio, and decided that Fleetwood Mac had to record in the home of Chicago blues before it shut down.

Working with Marshall Chess, Vernon prevailed upon Willie Dixon to organize the sessions, so Fleetwood Mac sat at the feet of the most-revered masters: Otis Spann, Muddy's piano player; Walter "Shakey" Horton, originally a teenage harp wizard; Honeyboy Edwards; J. T. Brown, who played his sax in Elmore James's Broomdusters; Buddy Guy as Guitar Buddy; S. P. Leary, Dixon's house drummer; and Willie Dixon himself.

From *Mick Fleetwood: My Life and Adventures in Fleetwood Mac*, Avon Books

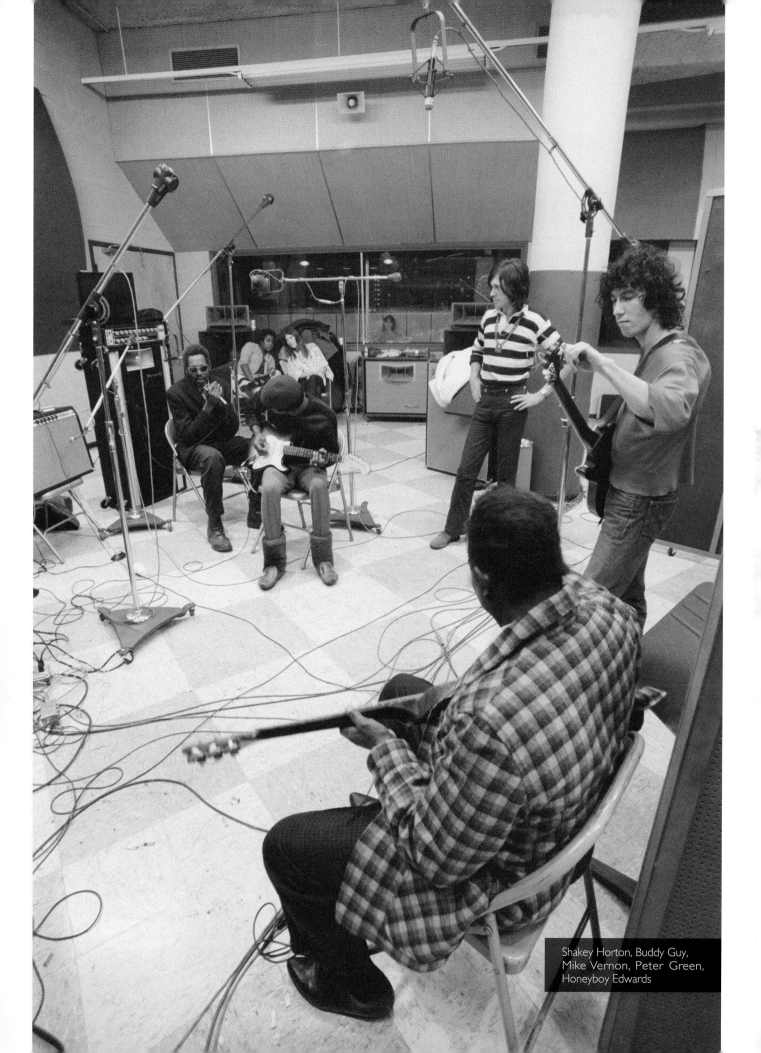

Shakey Horton, Buddy Guy,
Mike Vernon, Peter Green,
Honeyboy Edwards

Jeremy Spencer, Buddy Guy,
Mike Vernon

Mick Fleetwood, Otis Spann

Danny Kirwan, Peter Green, Otis Spann, John McVie

# JOHN SIEGER

There are some songs that act as calling cards. The writer/player/singer lays them on the table, and everyone but Hendrix and Django lay their hands down and go to some sad, defeated place in their heads. "Oh Well," written and played by Peter Green of Fleetwood Mac, is impossible. It's like five aces and, like that hand, unbeatable. First there are the super-slinky riffs, two main ones, played by Green and bandmate (and from what I see in the live video, future Muppet) Danny Kirwan. Any electric string bender genuflects before them and either learns to play the song (good luck!) or puts their guitar on Craigslist the next day. For those of you less guitar-cen-tric, there's Green's laughingly tossed-off vocal. The lyrics are wiseass and funny. Apparently he talks to God. I can't remember if I was gobsmacked or stupified—does it make any difference? So few songs do this, and Peter Green tossed it off, then dismissed it as a "throwaway riff."

Eat your hearts out, mere mortals; you've been schooled.

**John Sieger**
Songwriter, singer, and guitarist

John McVie, Peter Green,
Danny Kirwan

Honeyboy Edwards

Mike Vernon, Peter Green, Honeyboy Edwards, Buddy Guy, Stu Black, Jeremy Spencer, Willie Dixon, Shakey Horton

## DAVID "HONEYBOY" EDWARDS

David "Honeyboy" Edwards (June 28, 1915–August 29, 2011) was a well-known singer and guitarist from Mississippi. He received induction into the Blues Hall of Fame (1996); a Grammy Award, Best Traditional Blues Album (2008); and a Grammy Lifetime Achievement Award (2010), among numerous other honors
Official website: www.davidhoneyboyedwards.com

Shakey Horton, Buddy Guy, Honeyboy Edwards, Mike Vernon, Peter Green

Shakey Horton, Buddy Guy, Peter Green, Honeyboy Edwards

Shakey Horton, Danny Kirwan, Peter Green

Shakey Horton, Danny Kirwan, Peter Green

# BIG WALTER "SHAKEY" HORTON

Big Walter "Shakey" Horton (April 6, 1921–December 8, 1981). Willie Dixon called him "the best harmonica player I ever heard." He was posthumously inducted into the Blues Hall of Fame (1982). He was noted for his technique and tone (Wikipedia).

Shakey Horton, Peter Green

Jeremy Spencer, J. T. Brown

Shakey Horton, Danny Kirwan, Peter Green

Jeremy Spencer, Mike Vernon

# MARTIN CELMINS

### *Blues Jam at Chess* . . . Oh, the memories

Opening the gatefold sleeve of *Blues Jam at Chess* for the first time was a joyous moment for a geeky devotee of the Mac like me. No fewer than 105 35 mm contact-print-sized photographs to pore over and gain a sense of the session's vibe that day.

Studying those photos through a large magnifying glass, some geeky questions arose while noting instruments ("Why did Danny change to a Strat for Jeremy's numbers?"), amplifiers ("Why no sign of an Orange amp?"), and, most interesting of all, facial expressions ("Why does John McVie look so glum?").

I soon wrote to Blue Horizon, wanting to buy some enlargements, but, very politely, was informed that wasn't possible.

By the time the double album was released, I had been lucky enough to have seen the band three times in three very different kinds of venues. First, in the backroom of a large pub in Bradford, where, that night, the band got kitted out with the first Orange

amps ever made. This pub gig was just under three weeks before "Albatross" was released on November 22, 1968.

Second, in Manchester's Free Trade Hall on the closing night of B.B. King's April 1969 UK tour. Alas, the first house and not the second, at the end of which Peter, B.B., Duster Bennett, and others jammed together, and B.B. King, on behalf of *Disc,* presented the band with a silver disc for sales of "Albatross" exceeding 250,000.

Last, Redcar Jazz Club, playing in the Coatham Hotel's large ballroom five days before *Then Play On* came out on September 19, 1969.

So I was as familiar with two band members' onstage personalities as any fan could be. Nice guy Peter introduced the numbers and chatted to the audience, while zany Jeremy did his impromptu, funny, and sometimes rather rude impersonations and antics.

The inclusion of studio chat and false starts throughout *Blues Jam at Chess* struck me as an amazing bonus. It was the first time I heard Danny speak—sounding, understandably, a bit nervous and shy as he asks, "Can I start, all right?"

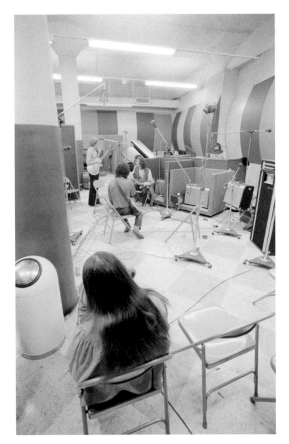

Danny Kirwan, Peter Green, John McVie

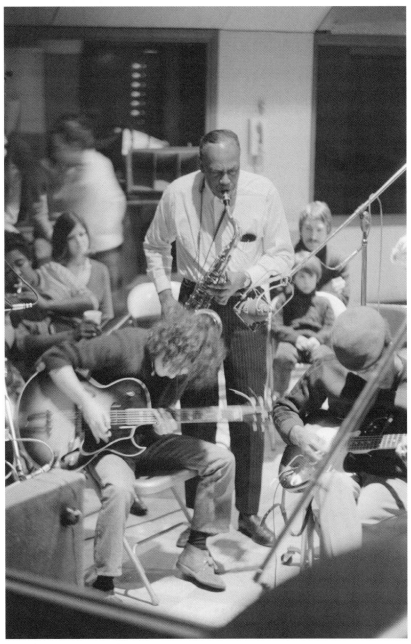

Jeremy Spencer, J. T. Brown, Buddy Guy

Hearing that, I visualized this blues boy wonder, still only eighteen, sitting there among much-older bluesmen who had created some of the music into which he had delved so deeply and had already interpreted in his own way.

A daunting prospect for him, perhaps, and yet his intro and playing on Jimmy Rogers's "World's in a Tangle" display the taste and restraint of a seasoned pro at least twice his age. And "Like It This Way" was the first outing on vinyl of the dual- and dueling-guitars sound that would become the band's calling card.

At the start of the session, Peter sternly asks Mike Vernon, "Do we have to have these lights on?," in a way that clearly indicates that this is a band leader *not* to be messed with. He once told me that his first impression when walking into the studio was that it reminded him of a school assembly hall and was not at all how he had imagined it would be.

As the musicians check their tuning after "I Held My Baby Last Night," Mick asks Mike, "Er . . . is this cymbal very, very loud still? Does this cymbal sound very tinny?" His accent struck me as more London-urban than the-shires-urbane tones I was expecting, given his rather upscale family background.

Then, almost at the end of the session and just before Peter's take on "Sugar Mama," there is some especially interesting and playful studio banter between Jeremy and him. It's to do with the fact that Peter sings, "Was it back in Philadelphia, woman?," whereas on Howlin' Wolf's best-known version (and Rory Gallagher's), the place is Louisiana.

Peter changed the lyric to Philadelphia in order to make the song more personal to him. How so? Well, apparently the previous weekend he had met and gotten on famously with one young lady when the band played two nights at Philadelphia's Electric Factory. And two months later, he was still singing Philadelphia and playing some impassioned solos at two concerts in Amsterdam, on February 28. Evidently, she was an unforgettable woman.

There were, and still are, three other standout tracks for me. "Ooh Baby" packs more punch than another of the band's Wolf-derived blues, "Long Grey Mare," from their debut album. John McVie's bass may well be one reason—Bob

Jeremy Spencer, Buddy Guy

Shakey Horton, Buddy Guy, Peter Green

Brunning depped for John on the "Dog & Dustbin" album track. What is also neat on "Ooh Baby" is the short top-strings phrase added in response to the classic "Killing Floor" riff's call—a simple but elegant idea that Peter told me he got from Chicken Shack's Stan Webb. How typical of his nature to give credit where credit is due.

The second standout is J. T. Brown's "Black Jack Blues." Willie Dixon's slightly out-of-tune bass bends sounded like no blues bass I'd heard before. Then in the midsong solo break, J. T. and J. S. duet seamlessly as Jeremy respectfully holds back in places so that his hero can shine. The raw overall sound conjured up two words in my rudimentary blues-lore imagination—juke joint.

Mac ended that Saturday, January 4, session with their wilder blues-rock take on Otis Rush's 1962 R&B version of the Perkins/Clark song "Homework." Otis Spann joined them on piano.

The following Thursday the band minus Mick joined Otis Spann at Tempo Sound Studios in New York to record *The Biggest Thing since Colossus*, an album that features

bluesmen—as opposed to blues-rockers—Peter and Danny at their tasteful finest.

That was then. What is rather perplexing since then is how Mike Vernon remembered Fleetwood Mac's general attitude about the Chess sessions when interviewed by *Record Collector* magazine around the time *The Complete Blue Horizon Sessions* series began to come out in 2005. Lamenting Blue Horizon's loss of its star attraction, he reflected: "I think what was underlying all of this [move to a major label] was that Fleetwood Mac decided they were no longer going to be a blues band. They had already moved into another musical area with 'Albatross,' and that may account for their couldn't-care-less attitude about the Chess sessions."

I disagree. Fleetwood Mac remained a blues band until their leader quit. True that by that time, rock ballads, heavy rock, and acid rock had been blended into their repertoire, but they were still *blues-based* and kept honing the blues segments of their gigs.

Returning to the Redcar Jazz Club on May 3, 1970, some three weeks before Peter left the band, what was the opener

Willie Dixon, Stu Black

of their three-hour set? An extended version of "Merry Go Round"—Peter's slow blues homage to B.B. King, taken from the debut album. Also that night, the winning number, measured in applause decibels, was Jeremy's rendition of Homesick James's "Got to Move"—a Mac favorite right from the start.

As for the band's attitude and approach to that day at Ter-Mar Studios, having listened again to the whole album and looked at the photos, it is Mick Fleetwood's recollection in the excellent 2010 BBC4 documentary *Blues Britannia: Can Blue Men Sing the Whites?* that nails it for me.

By this time, speaking in rather more-urbane tones, he said: "You know, *what* were they [the local Chicago musicians] thinking about us? You know. 'You're doing *our* stuff and . . . de-dur-de-dur . . . and coming into *our* world.' Luckily, it was a happy marriage because we paid attention and we knew, in truth, really how to behave."

Jeremy Spencer, Buddy Guy

**Martin Celmins**
Author: *Peter Green—Founder of Fleetwood Mac: The Authorised Biography*
Additional research: Mario Pirrone

Shakey Horton, Danny Kirwan, Peter Green

Jeremy Spencer, John McVie, Buddy Guy, Stu Black, Mike Vernon, Willie Dixon

Jeremy Spencer, Buddy Guy

# RICHARD ORLANDO

### SOUTH INDIANA, TAKE 2

Horton shows the band what he is going to be playing, and then illustrates what he would like to hear from Green by yapping out eight beats in a strange high-pitched voice. The remainder of the conversation is lost as the players begin fingering their instruments in anticipation.

The room then fills with the Green's guitar playing a jaunty hybrid of "Dust My Broom" and "Sweet Home Chicago." As if aligning himself to leap onto a moving horse that is running in circles around him, Horton feints once, twice, and then makes the leap, riding the riff like a rodeo trick rider.

From Richard Orlando, *A Love That Burns*, vol. 2, Smiling Corgi Press, 2018

Like Horton, Spann was best known (and to a certain degree, still is) for his support work, chiefly for Muddy Waters, but he was also a key session player at the Chess studios, sitting in with everyone from Howlin' Wolf to Chuck Berry. He was far more comfortable as band leader (or playing solo) than Horton and, although he began recording under his own name fairly late, managed to build a small, almost uniformly excellent library of recordings before his early passing.

Vernon's professional relationship with Spann stretched back to 1964, when he cut *The Blues of Otis Spann* as a staff producer for Decca.

Spann's vocals are like his playing: there is no filter between him and listener. He sings and plays from his heart, and there is never a sense of his forcing or shaping what comes out to fit a preplanned pattern.

From Richard Orlando, *A Love That Burns*, vol. 2, Smiling Corgi Press, 2018

The next night, Green got the opportunity to sit in with a local band at Pepper's Lounge on Chicago's South Side. It has been written that he was "escorted" there by Willie Dixon and Muddy Waters. Pepper's Lounge had been Waters's main venue for close to a decade at the time; he was just beginning to move into larger clubs and theaters, since his white audience was beginning to outgrow his traditional Black audience.

Otis Spann

Green took McVie's complaint, "Those guys made it quite clear that they didn't give a shit who we were," as one of the most exciting aspects of playing at Pepper's Lounge.

Green told Nick Logan, "If you can't play in a place like that, they are just waiting to let you know . . ."

The fact that his latest number had made number one on the English charts just a few weeks earlier would have meant nothing to the patrons in the club (they would not have heard it and probably would not have cared for it if they had), and Green would not have had it any other way.

These people had no idea *who* he was, *where* he came from, or what his reputation was back home; and they did not care. He would be judged solely on what he played that night and how he played it.

Green: "I could feel the whole attention of the club on me, and they were all clapping and shouting at the end. I was feeling so high, so proud after that performance. It was a lifelong ambition of mine to play before an all-Negro audience."

From Richard Orlando, *A Love That Burns*, vol. 2, Smiling Corgi Press, 2018

Dixon was a legendary figure on the Chicago blues scene; he was a man that everyone knew, and one who knew everyone worth knowing. He was rightly considered a "rainmaker." During the two decades prior to this session, he had written or produced an unprecedented string of hits and for the last six years had hired the talent for the American Folk Blues Festivals, in Europe. It was well known throughout the city that appearances on these shows had often led to many other recording and performing opportunities.

From Richard Orlando, *A Love That Burns*, vol. 2, Smiling Corgi Press, 2018

Buddy Guy, Peter Green

John McVie

Willie Dixon, Mike Vernon

Otis Spann, John McVie

Otis Spann

Jeremy Spencer, Buddy Guy

Mick Fleetwood, Shakey Horton, Danny Kirwan

Willie Dixon

Peter Green, Willie Dixon

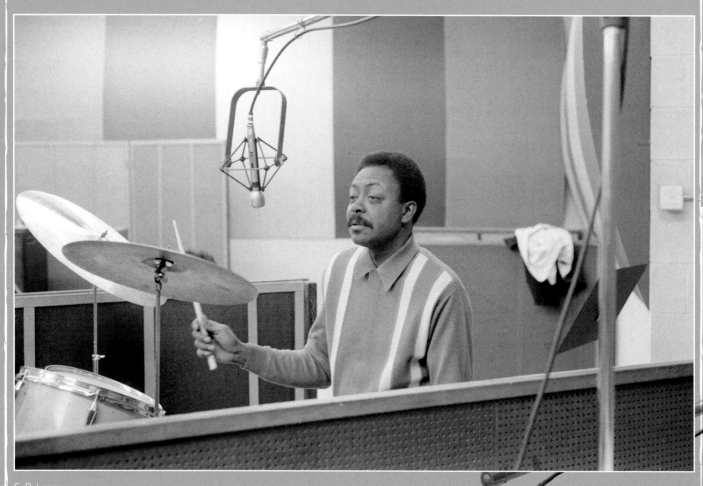

S. P. Leary

## S. P. LEARY

American blues drummer. Leary was inducted into the Rock and Roll Hall of Fame in 1995 and was also honored with the Key to the City of Dallas. He worked with Muddy Waters, James Cotton, T-Bone Walker, Lowell Fulson, and Howlin' Wolf, among others.

J. T. Brown

# J. T. BROWN

In Mississippi, J. T. Brown was a member of the Rabbit's Foot Minstrels and spent some time in Memphis, Tennessee, before moving to Chicago. He worked as a session musician for several artists and made some records on the Harlem label in the 1950s: "Round House Boogie" / "Kickin' the Blues Around," "Sax-ony Boogie," and "Dumb Woman Blues" were issued under various band names by Meteor Records in this period.

Brown later played and recorded with Elmore James and Howlin Wolf. He also recorded as a leader for several independent record labels, including Job and United.

Jeremy Spencer, Buddy Guy, J. T. Brown

J. T. Brown, Jeremy Spencer

Mike Vernon, Marshall Chess,
Stu Black

Peter Green, *back row*; Jeremy Spencer, John McVie, *front row*

Mick Fleetwood, Mike Vernon, Peter Green, John McVie

Stu Black, the man who engineered the session

Pressing-plant operator

Chess shipping department

Mike Vernon, Peter
Green, Danny Kirwan

Otis Spann, Mick Fleetwood

John McVie

Stu Black, Otis Spann, Mick
Fleetwood, John McVie

Mick Fleetwood

Guests with Peter Green,
Mike Vernon, John McVie

Peter Green

Jeremy's guitar

# BIBLIOGRAPHY

Celmins, Martin. *Peter Green: The Authorized Biography*. Sanctuary Pub. Ltd., 2003.

Fleetwood, Mick. *Love That Burns: A Chronicle of Fleetwood Mac*. Vol. 1, *1997–1974*. Surrey, UK: Genesys, 2017.

Fleetwood, Mick. *My Life and Adventures in Fleetwood Mac*. New York: Avon Books, 1991.

Orlando, Richard. *Love That Burns: Definitive Reference Guide*. Mt. Laurel, NJ: Smiling Corgi, 2017.

# INDEX

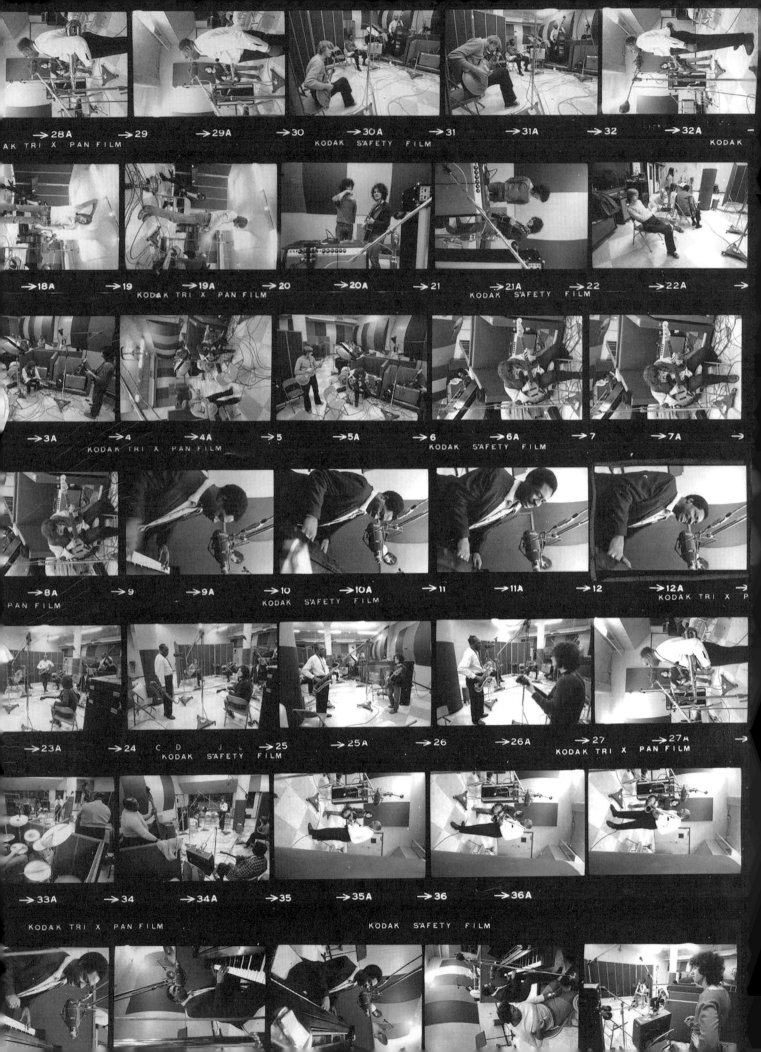